~ Betska K-Burr
Mind-Kinetics® Master Coach, Canadian author of many books including *The "God" in Coaching – The Key to a Happy Life*

In a world of confusion, destruction, suffering and distraction, this book shines through with a message of hope that an entirely different reality is possible. This book has the ability to touch every heart and inspire every mind because the ideas and concepts are rooted in Truth. Bring on Golden Age Politics. The time has come to change the world. Thank you, Kathy, for sharing this wisdom.

~ **Tammy Fry**
The Fry Family Food Co
Founder of Seed (Blog & Workshops)

The United Nations Sustainable Development Goal number five seeks to achieve gender equality and empower all women and girls and so does author Kathy Divine in her new book, *Golden Age Politics*. The book outlines a road map for her readers of how the world will be in much better shape as we go about raising the profile of the feminine attributes within all aspects of society. Ethical and compassionate decision making needs to shine through within our future leaders as we all strive for peace around the globe.

~ **Peter Thompson**
Australian voting citizen

Golden Age Politics

Inspired, ethical politics for
a peaceful, thriving world

Opinions expressed by contributors in this book are not necessarily held by the author, publisher or other contributors. Similarly, views expressed by the author are not necessarily held by contributors.

This publication does not purport to provide medical advice and readers should not rely upon any information which is contained in this publication for that purpose. Please consult an appropriate well-informed health professional if you are contemplating making a lifestyle or dietary change.

Published by Peace Era Publishing, an imprint of Australian Vegans

All enquiries to: info@kathydivine.com

Cover and interior design: Carolina Garzón

Editing: Penny Rowe, Mem Davis

ISBN: 978-0-9944462-1-3 (e-book)
ISBN: 978-0-9944462-2-0 (paperback)

NATIONAL
LIBRARY
OF AUSTRALIA

A catalogue record for this work is available from the National Library of Australia

Dedication

∞

This book is dedicated to all brave, noble souls
putting themselves forward to lead humanity into a compassionate,
ethical, peaceful, and sustainable world.

To my niece Gwen and nephews Teddy and Darcy,
this is all for you and the next generations of shining stars.
May you look forward to a bright future.

What others are saying about
Golden Age Politics

This book is a reminder of the possibilities for a more peaceful world and provides inspiration for becoming the ethical leaders we need.

~ **Rachael Morris**
Editor, *Nourish* **magazine**

Not into politics? This book is for you. Vegan author, Kathy Divine, gives us new ideas to be considered for a world we needed decades ago. This book implores you to shift your perception of what is possible when it comes to politics, leadership and spirituality. Kathy inspires us to move forward into a future that is bright with possibilities.

~ **Sara Kidd**
Author, Presenter & Recipe Developer
Food Columnist for *Vegan Food & Living Mag UK* **+** *Nourish Mag AU*

One word — hope. *Golden Age Politics* by Kathy Divine gives us hope for the future — a better future for Mother Earth and all her inhabitants. But what is this hope based on? The author provides a Golden Age political perspective where politics encompasses an engaged and informed public who choose political representatives who demonstrate ethical, responsible and compassionate decision-making across their portfolios.

The presentation of arguments and supporting evidence is balanced. On the one hand, the current *man*-made problems causing a human disconnect from the natural world and capitalism on steroids are stated, and on the other, the practical, innovative solutions to counter the resulting havoc are presented. There are so many nuggets of gold throughout this book, too many to name here but one that touched my political heart is the reference to the feminine; the vegan woman leading the way. Hallelujah! Chapter four affirms the desperate need for wise peace-loving vegan women to fix the toxic patriarchal global political systems. Through the stories of the female vegans profiled in this chapter, we learn how they are making a difference in the world now and into the future. The feminine at the helm is politics dipped in beauty — the beauty of peace for all beings on Earth.

Thank you Kathy for showing us what a better future could look like and how to achieve it. I highly recommend *Golden Age Politics* to those who yearn for a better world for our future generations and the planet we share. Moreover, to those who think they have nothing to contribute — yes you do, read this book and you will find the courage and conviction to share your ideas, talents and your voice for the improvement of local, national and global politics. As the author suggests: the future is ethical, responsible and compassionate leadership.

Thank you Kathy for this truly inspirational and aspirational book. Feeling Hopeful.

~ Suli Autagavaia
Author of *Animal Voices*

Kathy Divine's emotional but highly intelligent and astute writing is on display here in her sixth book, *Golden Age Politics*. This book deserves attention NOW — more so than ever before in our history. I am not usually into words like inspirational because I feel it's become a little over-used but I must say, *Golden Age Politics* is just that, an inspirational read.

It is not really a book about politics, though politics is in the title of the book. It is instead, a book offering advice to those who govern, to do so more ethically and with compassion.

Golden Age Politics is an open and honest book with clear instruction for all.

Bring on the Golden Age of Politics.

~ Lynn Bain
Director of Bodhi Events / Friends of Dalai Lama-Australia

Calling all women. Let's Rise and Lead together to bring in the ethical Vegan Law. That means putting an end to the abhorrent and cruel suffering inflicted upon humans and animals and Mother Earth. Babies born today will thank us for freeing them from the chains of hard core capitalism. Kathy Divine courageously touches our hearts and minds with the Truth to wake us up to conscious kindness and compassion.

Contents

Introduction

If you think politics is boring and not at all for the spiritually inclined, this book is for you. If even the word 'politics' triggers negative feelings within you: hang in there. This book may give you the hope you've been looking for. The political process can actually be one of the highest forms of spiritual service and has the potential to be innovative, interesting and fun. Seriously.

It's possible the political landscape will move in a positive direction and become a place where individuals and political parties of higher consciousness quite swiftly replace the current collection of old school leaders. Sound too good to be true? It isn't. Watch this space and read on for more powerfully positive news.

My vow in writing this book was to make politics interesting and inspiring for you, given that most people aren't interested in politics at all. Spirituality/religion and politics are considered the two big no-no's when it comes to social interactions because they are often divisive and highly personal subject matters. This book combines both in a way that aims not to divide, but to rather unite us in a shared vision for a better world.

Considering the overall global situation, this book may seem to be way ahead of the consciousness of humans currently inhabiting planet Earth. I don't intend for it to be seen as futurist and I have no interest in being branded as such. We've needed this style of politics yesterday, and the day before that, and even longer before that. We are facing the sixth mass species extinction and devastating climate change. We are in the middle of some *really* serious stuff as a species. So for this and many other urgent reasons, this book has come into being.

It's peace politics; the opposite of what we have now but absolutely within reach. As you may have already guessed, it's very blunt and straightforward, because there's no time to fluff around.

Golden Age Politics is *not* a utopian style monologue. It is a practical, highly doable blueprint for creating a system that is equitable, produces ethical outcomes, and establishes a sustainable planet made up of individual national governments that work together for the betterment of the multitude.

The leadership on this planet needs to change fast. There are glimpses of this kind of enlightened leadership occurring already. I hope more ethical and benevolent people will be inspired by those already doing it, to go into leadership positions and add to this emerging movement of forward-thinking leaders. Indeed, people like Greta Thunberg are pioneering this new brand of leadership, infused with truthful, ethical principles. Deep down in the depths of my being, I know there are many souls waiting in the wings for their opportunity to lead. *Golden Age Politics* is the toolkit you can utilise to prepare to become a member of this new wave of ethical leaders.

I received many confirmations to proceed with the book. One came from an unlikely source; former Australian Prime Minister Bob Hawke. To paraphrase, he said in an interview, "Progress doesn't come from saying we can't win, therefore we may as well stay in a cave." In other words, nothing gets done by hiding away, just because we think our ideas are not 'winnable' according to the thinking of the time.

I'd been thinking about this book, a blueprint for future political structure and wondering whether it would be too ahead of its time. The night after Bob Hawke's death, I was watching a playback of his life on the ABC, looking for signs to go ahead with this project. And there it was. He was a visionary and instigated a range of initiatives that were new and beneficial to the Australian people during his prime ministership. From that moment on, my resolve became stronger and my vision grander as I started to visualise the beginnings of a peaceful world governed by souls of higher consciousness.

Ultimately, it's up to humanity: you vote, you create your reality. You can bring in enlightened leadership either now or later. That is, if we even have the chance in later generations to realise this kind of world. Better make it happen now, to avert the current global environmental mess.

If your hope reignites and if this book renews your spirit and your inspiration to get out there and assist in co-creating the world you've always dreamed of, that's all I could ever wish for. Never give up. This world is in a temporary cycle of "what the...?" You are the new leaders of a kind, compassionate world. You are needed. Your voice and work is important in shaping the future of a planet grounded in kind, compassionate, intelligent, sustainable policy.

My first five books, my magazine *Australian Vegans Journal* and the Plant-Powered Women Leadership Conferences were the start of my own work regarding ethical leadership. *Golden Age Politics* examines the emergence of ethical leadership in global politics.

While embarking on your journey through the following pages, open your heart and mind to infinite possibilities. Remind yourself that the universe is vast, that we are all capable of tremendously great things, and together we have the ability to solve any issue that comes our way if we are open to genuine innovation and collaboration. These two concepts, applied sincerely and effectively, can take us to wherever we wish to go. I believe all of this to be possible when we have love in our hearts for all beings.

Thank you for going on this journey with me.

Let's begin.

Kathy Divine

In case you are wondering...

I am not a member of a political party and have no desire to enter into politics myself. This book is not part of my personal platform or future ambitions as a politician. The intention of this book is to support others with ethical leadership aspirations in politics and other areas of life including: business, non-profit, and community projects. It is also to assist voters to vote carefully and consciously.

Chapter One

An Overview of Golden Age Politics

Towards the end of my Bachelor's Degree in Commerce I came across a book completely by chance, all about alternative economics based on a shorter working week and a community approach to living based on sustainably sharing resources. It was around the same time I also discovered meditation. It all became part of the beginnings of my inner expansion of consciousness, and opening my mind to new possibilities. I wish I could remember the title of the book, but alas my memory fails me. However, what I've taken from it and from my further research on the topic over the last 23 years, is that we absolutely do not need to stick with the current set-up. There are far healthier, and more beneficial ways, of doing life.

Politics doesn't need to be boring and uninspiring

The political process is about people being voted or selected to serve their community. It is, at its highest, a position of service that should be humbly and carefully undertaken to ensure the most beneficial development and happiness of the society and people it serves.

Often, many people choose not to engage in politics because they perceive that elected representatives are not actually representing their needs and do not govern carefully nor humbly. This has created apathy and disdain among the populous of many nations as people don't see how their vote will change anything in a system where the choice of candidates is much the same in terms of motive and policy. Just the word 'politics', slipped casually into a conversation by those hoping to instigate intellectual conversation, can trigger a multitude of negative emotions, even anger, for some individuals and can spark a heated debate amongst otherwise tight groups of friends.

Social media is all about engagement. Every business, cause and influencer seeks the ultimate in engagement ability. Working out the exact formula of what will, or in many cases will *not* spark interest and constitute a high level of engagement for a brand, has become an art and a science. But what does this have to do with politics? Could a similar approach be beneficial? What is currently being done to get more people engaged in the political process? Is it even in the interest of governments to get more people involved and interested? Of course, the answers to these questions will vary from country to country.

If you're living in a country where the word *politics* is often reacted to negatively, I invite you to open up your mind a little whilst you read this book and notice how you are feeling as you process the ideas and concepts laid within. Rebranding politics as a community focused, positive process and career choice is one of the lofty goals of this book. I'm a passionate believer in the notion that politics has the potential, if done well, to be a form of high spiritual service to its community. I invite you to go on this journey with me and see if you can shift your perception of politics and what it could be, with ethical, dedicated leaders in place.

What is Golden Age Politics?

The book title *Golden Age Politics* could, to some people, sound like a phrase that is quite odd. Attempting to combine a spiritual phrase with politics is admittedly fairly unusual and out there, so what does it all mean?

In the spiritual counting of time, we are now in the beginnings of a Golden Age. In terms of politics, there are still remnants of the previous, negative age, lingering about, which is most evident in any policies you see coming from governments that are anything less than beneficial to all peoples, animals and the environment. Throughout this book I will cite examples to illustrate that Golden Age leadership is already starting to emerge around the globe. On an individual and community level there is lots of evidence to be found.

There are many who have spoken about our current time period as being the beginning of the Age of Aquarius, which is said to be associated with higher consciousness, increased concern for humanitarian issues, the ushering in of world peace, and other positive happenings. It's operating on a similar time frame to the end of the Mayan calendar, which ended in 2012, signalling not the end of the world, as many thought, but the end of an era. Spiritual Master and animal rights advocate Supreme Master Ching Hai has spoken in her lectures about this time period being the beginning of a Golden Age. References to the various ages, including the Golden Age, can also be found in historical writings from several sources, including Ancient Greece, Plato, and in the Indian epic *Mahabharata*.

There are certainly glimpses of positive progress to be seen around the world, such as an increase in people adopting a vegan lifestyle and the peace agreement signed between North Korea and South Korea. Effects of the negative cycle are still certainly being seen and felt in politics, but the energy and quality of a Golden Age is starting to pick up pace and momentum, which is typical of the beginning stages of any new age.

A golden age is characterised by peace and harmony, spiritual high consciousness, and an all-round good time to be had by all. These good times are fostered by notions of sharing, caring, being good to neighbours and sincerely wanting to have equality and just, fair treatment of everyone, including animals. It is also characterised by more gentle governing, with peace and harmony at the forefront of government decisions. It is also very common to see women and others with feminine traits leading countries, businesses, organisations and communities. Matriarchal systems and golden ages go hand in hand. Several women feature in this book as community leaders, golden age style.

If you're reading this book, I'm guessing you could be one of the many brave and noble souls who is active in co-creating the ushering in of this golden age world. If so, thank you for your work and your tireless efforts in spreading your positive, ethical energy to those around you. You *are* making a difference and it is all adding up to something very big, which is to come.

Glimpses of Golden Age Politics happening now

Although we are only a short way into seeing a fully realised golden age world, there are numerous examples worldwide, on all continents, that illustrate the shift is happening towards goodness and a compassionate way of thinking and implementing policy.

As the themes of a golden age include equality and a peaceful life for all, it is no surprise that groups dedicated to the protection of animals are beginning to come to prominence. In fact, in some parts of the world, these groups have even begun to become political.

Animal protection parties are starting to crop up all over the world with parties across Europe, the United Kingdom, Finland, Denmark, the Netherlands, Germany, in the United States and Canada, Brazil, Israel, Taiwan, and Australia — to name a few! The Animal Politics Foundation was founded in 2012 by the Dutch Party For The Animals, and is a network of animal welfare and rights focused political parties who network and share knowledge. The Dutch Party For The Animals have 80 elected representatives in various parliaments. Other countries with animal party elected representatives include the United Kingdom, Portugal, Germany, and Australia.

Legislation protecting animals exists in various countries, such as *The Animal Welfare Act 2006* in the United Kingdom. In the United States, the *Preventing Animal Cruelty and Torture Act* (PACT) was passed in 2019. Asia, Japan, and Taiwan have legislation for the care of specific species of animals. This is a good start, but much more inclusiveness and depth of legislation is needed to truly protect all animals from the wrath of human cruelty. This is something that Supreme Master Ching Hai has emphasised in her animal advocacy work for over the last three decades. She has said that although a golden age is beginning to emerge, much more effort and legislation is required to ensure animals are free to live their lives in peace and freedom.

Throughout the world, there is also a growing and concerted effort to protect our ecosystems and reverse the devastation of catastrophic climate change. Respect for, and a desire to nurture the natural world are also hallmarks of a golden age.

Jacinda Ardern, the Prime Minister of New Zealand, has been quoted as saying that worldwide economic growth should be considered 'an unnecessary evil' and that the world would be right to deprioritise it in favour of addressing more urgent environmental issues. Jacinda Ardern is not the only international leader attempting to safeguard the environment. Slovakian President Zuzana Caputova and Icelandic Prime Minister Katrin Jakobsdóttir are also both environmentalists of note, and, of course, female leaders in power. The return of the matriarchal system of governance is a sign of a returning golden age, and something discussed in more detail in Chapter Four. For now, I'd like to share a quote from Nicola Sturgeon, the First Minister of Scotland. While referencing the well-being before wealth concept, she said:

"I mentioned, a moment ago, our partner nations in the Wellbeing network: Iceland and New Zealand. It's worth noting, and I'll leave it to you to decide whether this is relevant or not, that all three of these countries are currently led by women."

And whilst we are considering the subject of strong women in high political positions, the current influence of Sahle-Work Zewde, the President of Ethiopia since 2018, is of powerful note. She is a firm believer in equal rights for all, is especially vocal about gender issues and has also held several positions within the United Nations including Head of the United Nations Integrated Peace-building Office in the Central African Republic (BINUCA).

Marianne Williamson in her book *The Politics of Love*, also talks about the importance of well-being and a 'sense of security' as the true definition of prosperity in addition to financial abundance.

There are a growing number of environmental projects taking place all over the world. In Germany, the government is aiming to close all of its coal-fired power plants by 2038. Africa is leading the way in banning plastic bag use, with 34 countries including Tanzania, Kenya, and Rwanda taking this issue very seriously. The government in the Philippines is hoping to pass a new law that makes it compulsory for citizens to plant trees. If passed, the law would mean that every student in the country would plant a minimum of ten trees before they were able to graduate.

Niulife, a coconut products business, have taken steps towards incorporating golden age principles into their business by revolutionising the way coconut oil is harvested, and are helping people in the process. The use of new technology enables production of the oil to be carried out on the Caribbean Islands where the coconuts grow, providing jobs for citizens there. All of the profits the company makes from the sale of the products are invested directly back into the islands, helping to provide jobs and reduce poverty. They are one of many ethical businesses doing their part to create a more sustainable, fairer world.

Within the Middle East there are elements of a golden age emerging, with the call for greater accountability, democracy, and equity from leaders and governments. Ethical leaders there include the Palestinian Animal League, who work tirelessly to help animals in need, as well as running vegan tours. There are also leaders like Pakistani activist Malala Yousafzai who is bravely speaking out for the education and empowerment of girls and women as a route to a more inclusive, balanced and healthy society.

Lastly, China and India have been reported as world leaders when it comes to tree planting, with NASA observing that the Earth is greener thanks to their efforts. India broke a world record by planting 50 million trees in just 24 hours, with 800,000 people in India coordinating together to achieve this feat. This is but one of many examples of united purpose that gives us hope of a brighter future on Earth.

Golden Age Media reporting on all the good news

As you can see, there are signs all over the world that a golden age has dawned. There are media outlets that are also emerging to share positive, ethically-based news with the world. Live Kindly, Plant-Based News, Vegan First, Jane Unchained, and Supreme Master Television are a few examples of the new wave of news outlets that are shining a light on forward-thinking leadership initiatives.

Freelance journalists such as Zoe Simmons are also playing their part in sharing inspiring news. Zoe writes here about the importance of ethics in journalism:

"It's easy to be ethical. No, really — it is. It's not caused by some kind of intricate magic potion. It's not something you just have or don't have.

"The reality is that *anyone* can be ethical; it's as simple as putting yourself into someone else's shoes, and asking, "Is this okay?"

"It's true: journalism often gets a bad rap for being unethical. But that's a stereotype I pride myself on undoing by throwing it *completely* out the window.

"Words have power — and as gatekeepers of the media, it's our role to be the voice for the voiceless, and to speak out about things that need to be spoken about. And as a journalist, I use that power to at least *try* to make the world a better place.

"You can't make a difference, I'm so often told. But in reality, I *can* make a difference. And in fact, I make a difference to every single person I write about. Like the woman whose father was being abused in an aged care facility, but no one believed her. Like the single dad with cancer who'd been cut off from his payments. Like the woman with an excruciating invisible illness who wanted to raise awareness about the reality of living with endometriosis.

"I put myself in *their* shoes. I take the time to find out the truth, and why things have happened, and how we can help. And I consider other potential ramifications — like how the story might affect their reputation, their future, and the people they know and love.

"Because it's not just a story: it's someone's life.

"Journalism is powerful. And I, for one, choose to use that power to make a difference."

Speaking of ethics...

Ethics. There are lots of wordy, academic definitions and schools of thought when it comes to ethics. Simply put, ethics is about being a decent person. Acting and thinking with your heart and soul. Your conscience. Being in touch with your true self and being unafraid of expressing it. It's about being real. The realest you can be. Ethical leadership is the future. People who care about global humanity, the animals, and the planet are what ethical leadership is all about. In these pages you will read a small sample of quotes from ethical leaders to illustrate the many different ways we can contribute to make the world a kinder place for all beings.

Peace first

Just to clarify, I'm not advocating at all for countries to change their political and economic systems, if it is already producing beneficial outcomes for people, animals and the environment. If your country does not operate under a political parties system, I'm not advocating revolt or revolution to change it. My philosophy is grounded one hundred per cent in peaceful politics. It seeks to add even more peace and unity to the world, and not to encourage violent or destructive upheavals.

A note on inclusion

It's time for the feminine energy to rise and lead. Whoever embodies that energy, we urgently need you to step forth, work together, and guide humanity forward. If you don't resonate with the masculine/feminine binary system and identify as something else such as non-binary, and also embody the same peace-loving, compassionate qualities that feminine energy is often known for, you are also among the ethical leaders we have been waiting for and deeply appreciate.

This is not forgetting men who are brave enough to embrace their softer, gentler side. You are also included in this leadership callout. When the phrase 'feminine leadership' is used in this book, it means let's put an end now to the dominance of aggressive, egotistical people running the world. All other contributions are highly appreciated. I love you for your individuality and powerful presence; simply being you. Your efforts in co-creating a peaceful, just world for all beings is hugely appreciated, no matter who you are.

I have so much love for absolutely everyone who is doing good work for themselves (self love is so important!) and the world. Being inclusive is very important to me, together with communicating the importance of the feminine to rise and lead. Thank you, every single one of you, for embracing these ideas with an open heart and mind while realising that one book can't possibly cover every complexity facing humanity right now. *Golden Age Politics* is simply my little contribution among many, many others.

In the next chapter we will examine various policy portfolios and where the golden age goodness can be found within them. If you turn the page and start reading the next chapter, you are reading more than the average person does after picking up a book. According to statistics, the majority of books purchased are not read beyond the first chapter. Please join me in the next chapter so I can continue to share more hope and inspiration with you about the beautiful world we can co-create together.

Chapter Two

Golden Age Policy

In this chapter I'll discuss several key policy areas. With so much ground to cover, I've chosen policies that are significant to the pressing issues this planet is facing, like food shortages, environmental concerns, and other issues that are frequently brought up in election campaigns such as employment and economic growth. I'll discuss current policies that are not serving us well as a global society, examples of Golden Age policy being implemented now, and examples of policy ideas we could adopt in the future.

All of these policy headings deserve their own books, as each deserves detailed and considered treatment, rather than the mere snapshot presented here. There are books in the reference list that will give you more detailed information for your consideration.

I'll open by saying I'm not an expert on any of the policy topics discussed in this chapter, all I know is that 'business as usual' is getting us nowhere. I've enlisted the assistance of professionals for some topics, to write brief overviews here. Please see their biographies at the back of the book to follow their work in more detail, if you're interested in delving deeper into one of these topics.

Underpinning the policy ideas in this chapter are the following considerations: this chapter and the rest of the book is in no way advocating for socialism, or capitalism, or any other particular economic system. Emphasis and debate is placed too much on which economic system is the best. It really isn't as crucial as the level of consciousness of the people. A high fairness and kindness quotient will render any economic system a success. Greed and corruption within any system will create a rotten country. It's the hearts and the ethics of the people within any system that is paramount. Although, it's really unlikely that exponential consumerism would be the system of choice in an enlightened society as it goes against principles of sustainability and caring for natural surroundings.

Forget about focusing on economic frameworks and being preoccupied with the fallacy of scarcity. Seek to build communities and the health of a nation in all ways (for people, animals and the environment). Resources are now scarce only because humans have not lived in harmony with their environments and other animal species. Lack of water and food is not a normal state of being for any healthy functioning society. Humans have dominated over the Earth and other species of flora and fauna, creating catastrophic conditions for ecosystems all over the world. There's no scarcity when everything is in balance. *I repeat:* **Scarcity as an economic principle is utterly flawed. Abundance *is* the natural order of things.**

Okay, let's get into the policy details.

Future of food policy and subsidies

The future of food is vegan. Why is that? Because it's a sustainable way to feed the ever-growing global population. It takes less resources (water, land) than animal agriculture. Factory farmed livestock are often fed soy beans and then that livestock is fed to humans. Smart business is always about finding ways to skip out the middle person to cut costs. The same should apply to feeding humans. Skip the middle manager, eat the soy beans, humans.

The smart farmers, noticing the shift towards plant-based eating, aren't waiting for governments to provide subsidies, they are getting out now by transitioning to the ever-growing market for all things plant.

Dairy Free Down Under are one such family-run farming business in Australia. While governments insist on propping up dying industries, forward-thinking farmers are taking matters into their own hands and finding success in the burgeoning plant-based food business sector.

I attended a talk by Bob Burke from Natural Products Consulting at the Naturally Good Expo in 2019, in Sydney Australia, where he talked about the natural health products trends in the US. Bob said it's all about 'plant-based everything', meaning plant-based food products of all types are continuing to be hot items that people are demanding. As more and more people become aware of the health, environmental and other benefits of vegan lifestyles, food production will shift to meet this change in mindset. We only need to look at where the billionaires are investing to know what's what. Jeff Bezos, Bill Gates and Richard Branson are three who have invested in plant-based businesses over the past few years.

Katrina Fox is the author of *Vegan Ventures: Start and Grow An Ethical Business* and the founder of VeganBusinessMedia.com. I asked Katrina for her comment on the rise and rise of vegan business:

"Since 2014, as a result of increasing public awareness about the health benefits of plant-based eating, the devastating impact of animal agriculture on the environment, and the immense and abhorrent suffering inflicted on non-human animals for our consumption, there has been a massive growth in vegan and plant-based products, services, and businesses.

"Global sales of plant-based meat, fish and dairy alternatives continue to be on an upward trend. Vegan meat company Beyond Meat launched its IPO in 2019, with initial return on investment appearing positive for early investors.

"Even multinationals not known for their ethics are jumping on the bandwagon: Nestlé is bringing out plant-based food products; Tyson, one of the largest meat companies in the US, has done the same and rebranded as a 'protein' company; and vegan brands are being bought by large conglomerates such as Unilever and pharmaceutical companies.

"The jury is still out as to whether this rise in 'vegan capitalism' will make life better for animals and people, and save the planet. Certainly making animal-free products both physically and financially accessible to the masses is essential and these large corporations have the infrastructure to facilitate this.

"For real change to occur though, we need governments to step up and commit to supporting a transition to a plant-based economy. Phasing out subsidies to the animal agriculture industry is likely to be one key step, along with providing support, such as tax breaks, grants and other incentives, to vegan and plant-based businesses, particularly those with a strong commitment to human rights and sustainability — in other words, rewarding businesses and brands that are ethical, and penalising those that are not.

"Support must be provided to animal farmers, slaughterhouse workers, and associated businesses involved in the manufacture of animal-based products and services to help them transition into new jobs, careers, and businesses."

Feeding plants to people is not only efficient resource allocation, it turns out it's great for job creation and economic growth too. Conversely, for a deeper look at the inefficiencies of the animal agriculture industry, *Meatonomics* is a detailed examination of the meat industry in the US and how far the government will go with subsidies to prop up an unprofitable, cruel industry.

Bob Ratnarajah is a speaker, coach and consultant to businesses who want to 'be the change in business' and adapt to the 21st century conscious consumer. He founded Beta Catalyst Consulting, with a vision to 'enable good business to be greater, to change the world sooner'. He says no one is happy with money alone — yet that's how we measure a business's success today:

"Let's change the paradigm by measuring areas of a business related to its **purpose**, how it treats **people**, and the **planet** (impact), all while helping the business achieve maximum **profitability**. To ensure these goals are achieved, businesses need **precision**. I've coined the term *Organisational Wellbeing* to describe these five pillars. By tracking these qualitative attributes with a scorecard, business leaders have the tools to thrive."

Looking after nature, animals, and people while also making money; sounds like a sustainable plan that's also good for the economy. Thought leaders like Mr Ratnarajah will be increasingly in demand as big businesses realise that business-as-usual isn't going to work for much longer.

Vegan Australia, a national vegan advocacy charity, has begun research into a 100% vegan agricultural system for Australia. As part of this, they have looked at how land currently used for animal farming could be repurposed for other activities, such as growing extra fruit, vegetables and crops, carbon farming, regrowing bushland and forests, and restoring the rangelands.

Across the bay, the New Zealand Health Ministry showed forward-thinking, compassionate leadership through its Sustainability and The Health Sector Report by encouraging plant-based eating, stating that, "Producing meat (particularly red meat) is resource intensive and has a larger carbon footprint than producing plant-based protein alternatives."

Animal rights and welfare

While we are on the subject of food, I'll segue into the policy regarding the treatment of animals. Exploitation of any kind towards animals should be illegal, which obviously includes killing animals for food and clothing and everything else in between. All animals deserve to live in peace and freedom. A UK barrister Michael Mansfield suggested in 2019 that eating meat will one day be outlawed, reflecting the trend towards ethically responsible consumption. It will indeed happen eventually worldwide as the consciousness of humanity rises.

Economic Growth

Putting an end to fear-based 'jobs and growth' slogans

In stark contrast to the current Australian government's broken record slogan of 'jobs and growth', New Zealand Prime Minister, Jacinda Ardern, has boldly declared that economic growth isn't as important as the wellbeing of the citizens and the sustainability of the planet. Basically, economic growth does not equal happiness and, in urgent times like these, environmental concerns trump good economic figures, in terms of where our priorities should be. Bhutan has long been a leader when it comes to this concept, with its emphasis on gross national happiness. As the name suggests it is an index that is used to measure the happiness of a population.

Having a job does not equal happiness

The casualisation of the workforce means economic growth, measured as GDP, does happen. But workers employed on a casual basis have insecure employment and no access to the benefits enjoyed by workers who are permanently employed. Technically, casual employees have a job and are contributing to economic growth (through their productivity), but not in a way that brings stability, security, or wellbeing to that employee. It does, however, often bring anxiety and fear of the future. Not healthy.

So when voting in the next election, please look behind the slogans and ask candidates for the complete story, because the actual outcomes in terms of standard of living can differ greatly to the expectation. This is why Ardern et. al.'s approach is preferable; it's honest and achieves beneficial outcomes for the people, which in the long term, actually means economic growth will occur anyway. Happy and healthy workforces are productive workforces.

A happy, healthy society where individuals work in jobs they love results in innovation, invention, creativity, and yes; higher productivity and economic growth. Look after the people, animals and the environment first and foremost and the economy takes care of itself. We don't need to choose economic growth *or* sustainability. We can have it all. Focus on wellbeing first and industries that are sustainable, future-proofed and cruelty-free. It solves everything. Sustainable energy and plant-based markets are the new markets of the future. Governments investing in and supporting these industries will experience all of the positive outcomes of a golden age for their country.

Scarcity is an illusion. This illusion is so ingrained in the human psyche, it bears repeating. We can all live abundantly if we get our priorities sorted out. This doesn't have to include adhering to any spiritual principles such as the Law of Karma. It's not even necessary to believe in it. From a scientific perspective alone, doing the right thing ethically by humanity, animals and the environment is the long term solution to creating a happy, healthy and safe world for all beings.

The alternative is what we already have: a high level of stress and a lifestyle-diseased population because we are holding up economic growth as some kind of god to bow down to, or else we perish. We are perishing under this regime already! This system isn't sustainable on any front in the long term.

Exploring the degrowth movement

While doing the research for this book, I came across the *degrowth movement*. Degrowth refers to reducing economic growth in order to reduce carbon dioxide emissions. Certainly, the movement towards minimalism has numerous benefits to the environment and I'd agree that certain industries such as fossil fuels and animal agriculture should degrowth to zero and be eliminated as sources of production and GDP.

Working less, and therefore creating less economic growth, is certainly an interesting concept that needs further exploration to ensure the poor don't get poorer. Under the degrowth system, the introduction of a universal living wage is suggested to counteract this potential problem.

Economic growth should be taught as an educational subject with respect to future sources of growth and identifying dying industries as unsustainable sources of growth. Animal agriculture, dairy and coal are sources of growth that belong in the past and technically shouldn't be considered as economic growth potentials. When looking at the bigger picture, they are actually anti-growth sources. In the long run, considering these industries cause either poor health and/or poor environmental outcomes, they actually *cost* the economy money, so they are not sustainable sources of growth. Anyone that suggests the opposite is clearly either funded by these industries or has some kind of investment in them. Or they simply don't care either way. Apathy is a problem among both voters and some elected representatives. Vote for someone who cares about sustainable economic growth sources, because the planet depends on you caring and you voting in people who care. No excuses. This is not negotiable.

The cost to the health system of certain medical conditions that are diet (meat, eggs and dairy) related is unnecessary government budget wastage. Instead of supporting dying industries, backing healthy plant-based food manufacturing and implementing public health campaigns that highlight the benefits of plant-based eating are two ways governments can save money. That money can then be used to solve social issues like homelessness, more services for Indigenous populations, and housing affordability. These are issues facing many nations and are just a few examples where government money could be better spent. See *Australian Vegans Journal* (*Volume Two)* for Michael Dello-Iacovo's article about budget spending on public health campaigns and the potential savings to government.

Every person and their pooch knows that coal is bad for the environment.

This is another net negative economic growth factor that should be eliminated. In any case, this issue is losing favour with voters (except for local voters where heavy scare campaigning has led to them fearing lack of employment because of closing coal mines), so it's an extra level of motivation to drop them as industries.

Environment

"To our utter dismay, without contributing to environmental destruction, we are confronted with a situation where Bangladesh is one of the most climate-vulnerable countries in the world."

Sheikh Hasina

Prime Minister of Bangladesh

Humanity who seeks to dominate over nature and manipulate everything will see to their own downfall. There's no way around it. Choose to share, care and help others and see how this planet renews itself.

The next section was written by Jenny McCracken, a visual artist who has been a climate activist for 12 years. Creative solutions to pressing problems are something we need more of. There are lots of lawyers in parliaments, who tend to be very analytical in nature. We certainly need them among our elected representatives, but we also need to balance the analytical with the creative and innovative, so in writing this book, I was conscious of inviting both sides of the brain (left and right), to see what they could contribute. Jenny has presented both the statistics and creative solutions here for us to consider.

Ethical Environmental Policy
Bringing the soul back into our relationship with the land.
A radical rethink of our approach to environmental policy.
by Jenny McCracken

There is almost universal agreement, across all scientific disciplines, that our oceans, ecosystems, natural diversity, and climate stability are at the point of critical destabilisation, and perhaps collapse.

Consumerist economic culture, as the dominant driver of the current global economic paradigm, now treats everything as a commodity. Caught up in this frenzy of consumption, we enslave animals, people and nature for the overriding purpose of making money. We humans, in the pursuit of creating and controlling an endless stream of consumable resources to sell to one another, have destroyed 10 million square kilometres of the planet's forests in the last 100 years, over-fished or fully exploited approximately 87 per cent of the fish in our seas (according to the FAO), and extensively depleted the health of the earth's arable soils. We have done this with little or no thought for the lives with whom we share the planet, human or otherwise, and with little or no appreciation of what this profligate consumption leaves for our descendants.

In order to halt this global destruction, we need to radically, but simply, rethink our relationship with all life — including ourselves. Nothing less than that will allow us to bring about the change in consciousness necessary to harmonise our activities with nature, and rebuild an environment that is stable, balanced and resilient.

In so many ways it is clear that our relationship with the natural world is broken. If it were a marriage, we humans would be the abusive, narcissistic party, simply using our spouse as a slave to our needs and taking what we need from her; stripping her naked and leaving her broken and battered so that we could profit at the expense of any future we may have together, not to mention the future of our children.

Yet humanity's relationship with nature has only become this globally unbalanced within the last century of our hundreds of thousands of years of existence on the planet. There is increasing acknowledgement of the highly developed agriculture the First Nations peoples of Australia practiced in this land, without causing environmental collapse. Vast plains of naturally cultivated grains were described by explorers such as Sturt, on first contact with the peoples in the west of what is now New South Wales, with other descriptions of fields of native yams being harvested by women and gathered into storage areas of many tonnes for later use. Clearly the Aboriginal way of life was maintained fruitfully, healthily, and continuously on this most arid of continents for about 80,000 years.

Across the globe, the documentation of first contacts with Indigenous inhabitants almost universally describe robustly healthy and happy populations, right up until their land and economy are destroyed beneath the herds of colonising beasts and humans. These animals and settlers brought diseases, destruction, and literally 'ground breaking' methods of farming. Here in Australia, the result — a mere 200 years into this wave of invasion — is that we have the highest rate of mammal extinction in the world, having lost 34 species, and a further 29 species of birds in that period, according to John Woinarski, of Charles Darwin University. Many more are threatened. The total quantities of flora we have lost is unknown, as many likely disappeared before ever being documented.

What is absolutely clear is that so many of us have lost our connection with nature, we have ceased to see the natural environment, in all its richness and diversity as something to respect, to be in awe of, to be grateful for. So many people now grow up in an urban environment, their experience of nature being limited to manicured lawns, house plants and 'pests'. There is no deep living relationship with the natural world; the wild places and creatures who inhabit them. Without this we are unable to recognise the irreducible value of an intact, balanced environment, to recognise we depend on it for the very survival of all life as we know it. Overlay that with the psychology of consumption as the *raison d'etre* of modern existence and you have the recipe for our current predicament. We urgently need to reconnect with the life around us, and to understand that all life is one. Protecting the living environment protects us.

Albert Einstein made an astute observation over one hundred years ago, that, "Nothing will benefit health or increase chances of survival on Earth as the evolution to a vegetarian diet." This can be modernised to, "Nothing will increase the health and chances of modern human society surviving as the evolution to a universal vegan philosophy of compassionate non-violence". The vegan philosophy, that acknowledges the right of every sentient being to live a life free from exploitation by humans, is the only platform that guarantees integrity and consideration for all life. It is the only approach that ensures that the intrinsic value of any life form will be taken into consideration for its own sake in any decisions regarding human land use, land restoration, or environmental alteration.

Investigative journalist and author George Monbiot, in his book *Feral,* makes a clear case for restoring and preserving the wild places around us not only to remind people of the majesty of our natural world, but to preserve the intricately balanced web of life that gives our environments resilience in the face of catastrophe. The core of this transition is learning to work with equal respect for every sentient being's right to live out their natural life and inclinations, in a way that precludes self-serving use and abuse by humans.

To do this we need a revolution in environmental policy and practice. So what might that look like?

The first thing would be acknowledging the emergency situation as a matter of primary importance. The climate and environmental crisis is the situation that will impact everything else: food, water, health, national stability, jobs, the global economy and refugees. Then, crafting policy along the lines of what is known in the United States as a 'Green New Deal', but building into it the vegan philosophy of non-violent compassion to facilitate this economic and environmental transformation.

Most radically, the Environment Minister needs to replace the Treasurer as the position of highest importance. This critical decision-making position would be supported and facilitated by all the other portfolios. The whole national budget would need to be assessed in terms of how it contributes to the environment budget. Shifting economic focus away from the industries that negatively affect the environment requires a rapid increase of alternative clean industries. This process would mean many jobs becoming redundant, with new jobs created and business growth empowered to rebuild an environmentally ethical economy.

All of the steps towards this transformation need to be urgently implemented, such as transitioning agriculture to replace all animal industries with plant-based food production, and facilitating crop production to supply protein directly to humans. In addition, organic, non-artificially fertilised farming (creating healthier soil and facilitating soil carbon storage) is paramount. De-stocked land can be used for regenerative re-wilding and further carbon storage. All waterways need to be restored to optimum function and rebuilt in ways that can withstand the greater flow of larger storms, so that the water is held in the land naturally as long as possible. Higher and healthier water tables mean healthier and more resilient plants and trees, and stability of water movement through its cycles of transpiration. As water is retained in the soil and vegetation, the whole environment becomes healthier and stronger, while less vapour hangs in the atmosphere, amplifying the weather systems and the greenhouse effect.

Subsidies would work to support the positive growth areas of renewable energy generation, plant-based food supplies, and restoration of forest and natural habitat wherever possible, creating a linked network of corridors between existing areas of virgin and newly regenerated natural bushland. This would be done by incentivising and genuinely supporting farmers from the animal agriculture sector to transition smoothly to new sustainable and ethical industries.

Tax incentives can be used to encourage farmers to transition away from destructive animal industries and convert to plant-based, organic farming or new carbon-sequestering hybrid industries. Interestingly, Australia is particularly well placed for many farming communities to begin utilising solar power to provide energy, and husbanding the local water and land resources in order to restore and revegetate degraded soils and waterways, thus supporting communities to develop new industries that are climate resilient.

There are advanced technologies in operation now that are incredible game changers. One example is the growth of high nutrient density algae, which is then turned into biochar, while generating electricity. This brilliant system generates enough energy to supply its own needs, and to power one hundred greenhouses in any weather or circumstance. The fertiliser and biochar produced is a super organic soil treatment, shown to be powerful enough to revolutionise our organic food production, energy supply, and water use, should it be widely adopted. This is a revolutionary way of making solar power.

We have roughly 60 years of tillable soil left in the world, if we continue farming in the current paradigm. With heavy dependence on chemicals to grow our food en masse for the supermarket chains, the goal of big agricultural giants is to keep farmers locked into a seed purchase, weed killer/insect killer cycle from which they cannot escape. Urgent transition to a new way of living in and with nature is critical to survival of life on Earth as we know it.

The ideas and solutions presented in this article aim to raise awareness of the issues and the urgency that we are faced with currently. With a sincere acknowledgement by governments worldwide of the challenges we face and a corresponding commitment to take sustainable and meaningful actions, we will together restore this planet to its rightful beauty and majesty.

∞   ∞   ∞

There is the science and then there is the spiritual oneness with nature. Open your heart and contemplate on the following quote from Thich Nhat Hanh, a vegan monk and dedicated environmentalist:

"There is no phenomenon in the universe that does not intimately concern us, from a pebble resting at the bottom of the ocean to the movement of a galaxy millions of light years away. All phenomena are interdependent. When we think of a speck of dust, a flower, or a human being, our thinking cannot break loose from the idea of a self, of a solid permanent thing. We see a line drawn between one and many, this and that. When we truly realise the interdependent nature of the dust, the flower, and the human being, we see that unity cannot exist without diversity. Unity and diversity interpenetrate each other freely. Unity is diversity, and diversity is unity. This is the principle of interbeing.

"If you are a mountain climber or someone who enjoys the countryside and the forest, you know that the trees are our lungs outside of our bodies. Yet we've acted in a way that's resulted in millions of square miles of land being deforested, and we've also destroyed the air, the rivers, and parts of the ozone layer. We're imprisoned in our small selves, thinking only of having some comfortable conditions for this small self, while we destroy our large self. If we want to change the situation, we must begin by being our true selves. To be our true selves means we have to be the forest, the river, and the ozone layer*.

"If we visualise ourselves as the forest, we will experience the hopes and fears of the trees. If we aren't able to do this, the forests will die, and we lose our chance for peace."

Reprinted from *The World We Have: A Buddhist Approach to Peace and Ecology* (2008) by Thich Nhat Hanh with the permission of Parallax Press, Berkeley, California, www.parallax.org.

Although the issue of the ozone layer is not as current and urgent as climate change due to it partially healing, its effects are still being felt and emphasises that whatever we do to the planet in the past, is difficult to fully undo without great efforts. I've put an interesting article about this in the reference list about how the ozone layer hole and climate change issues interact.

Gun control

Seinfeld fans will likely remember the episode where the book *War and Peace* gets renamed *War What Is It Good For?* by Elaine, prompted by Jerry's joking suggestion. But seriously, what is war good for, except to make rich people richer by selling guns to the vulnerable, the misguided, or the corrupt?

As an Australian who has been privileged to visit the United States, I have an affection for much that the U.S has to offer, from their cool television shows and films, to their exceptional customer service, noted for its conscientious approach and friendliness. However, from the news we now have increasing access to courtesy of the Internet, even an outsider can see that the US is in trouble.

There seems to be too much focus on profits and very rapid growth in all ways, and not enough caring about people, animals and the environment in the process. Although, this is arguably almost a global phenomenon, since hardcore capitalism has grown and prospered under strong US influence and dominance. This is particularly true regarding the US military-industrial complex, the creation of ever more deadly weapons, and the defence and promotion of personal firearm ownership. I always pray for the US and have deep faith in the many people there working towards healing the fractures in their society. Organisations like March for Our Lives (https://marchforourlives.com) and Americans Against Gun Violence (https://aagunv.org/) gives me hope that somehow they'll be okay.

Within adversity there is opportunity. At a time when the US leads the developed world in firearm violence and death, there is the chance to unite as a nation that prioritises peace and the surrendering of guns, rather than perpetuate an unnamed civil war whose death toll is already in the tens of thousands per decade. In a country that professes strong Christian values, defending the constitutional right to bear arms defies Jesus' call to love one another (John 13:34), in the most desperately tragic way.

American citizens must unite in a call for reform of gun ownership, because true freedom and peace comes from disarmament. Constitutional rights which underwrite violence maintain a frightened and angry population. In response to a particularly devastating mass shooting in Australia in 1996, the then government bought back many of the guns from private citizens. Therefore, most Australians do not live in fear of gun violence. I'm not suggesting that Australia — or any other developed nation with stricter gun control — is free of violent crime, but we are safer as a result of not having so many gun owners to contend with. While protection of individual rights is admirable, your right to real peace and safety before the right of people to shoot each other is a right worth pursuing, wouldn't you agree?

A healthy society doesn't require a heavily armed community. To paraphrase Confucius, world peace starts with firstly individual peace, family peace, neighbouring peace, national peace, and then world peace. A society living in constant anxiety and fear of each other goes against our true nature as interconnected beings. Golden Age worlds don't have guns because they don't need them. This isn't a fantasy goal, it can happen. And it must happen if we are to remain viable, and especially if we are to evolve as a global community. Something has to change, and quickly.

Enough with the guns already. As one of the most advanced nations on many indicators, it is sad to see the US so far down the list of peaceful nations.

Humanitarian aid

It's not complicated. Those that have more should give more. We are all One; sisters and brothers of many lands. Assist the needy. Care about others. Politics should be non-partisan when it comes to this policy portfolio. It should be all about serving unconditionally. Helping those in need without anyone expecting anything in return.

If I start intellectualising this topic just because that's what's expected or acceptable for an author writing on this topic, I'm simply not being authentic. When we deeply love and respect each other and are sensitive to suffering, we can work things out between nations, as friends. This goes for giving aid, creating peace, and everything else. Love is the most powerful force in the universe. It's also the most natural of emotions and way of being. We are love. I did reference reading of intellectual and academic books but they didn't convince me to change my perspective, even when I tried really hard to do so. My default solution is love and there's nothing I can do about it. Those who are aligned and sensitive to that energy will understand and feel in tune with this approach and others won't, and that's perfectly fine because we all have different way of reaching different people and audiences and different ways of solving the same problems.

Education

One thing all children deserve to learn is a thorough understanding of the electoral and governing processes of their state and/or country, and how they can participate fully. The wider issue of education is vast and complex. The brainwashing of children that occurs within our modern education systems is deep and extensive. In subjects like history, geography, and economics there are more obvious components of propaganda weaved throughout the curriculum, but almost no subject is free from the influence of vested interests.

For tertiary courses, where students are encouraged to do their own research, they can often find the culture and scope of their discipline is sufficiently constrained to discourage thinking that deviates from established norms.

Publication and/or employment within academic communities is heavily influenced by industry expectations, profitability, and politics, which means that those who further these interests determine curricula and research agendas.

There's never been a more relevant time to revamp the education system. Children nowadays are more exposed to information than ever before. Outdated syllabuses that fail to engage and respect students do not prepare young people for life in the contemporary world.

The New Human by Mary Rodwell is without a doubt a book that's ahead of its time in many respects, and her chapter about the education system is really worth looking at for anyone involved with education policy. According to Rodwell, the children of today and those coming after them are different. They are more highly attuned and evolved spiritually, and need education that suits their grand missions and aspirations. They also need support and understanding in the sense that, despite their young age, there will be many who are wise beyond their years; here to do great and noble things. Treating these great souls like they are ignorant is a disservice to both them and the planet they seek to assist.

Children are in a pure state and thus can access their unfiltered and untarnished intuition. The education system needs to acknowledge and recognise this first of all, and then seek ways to support children with a new way of learning and developing. It's easy to blame children for poor grades and for dropping out of school. Harder to dig a little deeper and recognise what needs fixing.

The number of top entrepreneurs and business people who dropped out of university to start their projects is a sign that formal education may hold some people back from realising their dreams. Personally, I've learnt more about business from people without degrees and in a much shorter space of time than the tedious three years it took to obtain a commerce degree. High school was also a mind-numbing drag to get through, to get the grades, to get a university place. The whole process was yawn central.

We must also offer more to the extra sensitive kids, who are growing in numbers. Mary Rodwell calls them the 'letter people', to denote the labels these kids and adults are given like ADHD and ASD (autism spectrum disorder). These children and adults need appropriate accommodations in order to function and thrive in an increasingly overwhelming world.

This is also the case for other sensitives whom psychologist Elaine Aron has termed, 'highly sensitive people', which she states includes up to 20% of people. When we look at kids who can't cope in school or who start displaying disruptive behaviours, we need to see where the source of irritation and potential sensitivity issue is.

Nations with a sincere intention to support children in bringing out their full potential and talents, will actively seek to create environments that support and engage these wonderful souls. That is the emphasis of my project 'Ask The Aspie' which seeks to bring autism awareness, acceptance, and solutions to the wider community, particularly in schools and employment settings. There is much untapped talent and ability within children and adults on the autism spectrum. In many cases, as for climate activist Greta Thunberg, they just need the circumstances, environment, and opportunity to share their vision and unshakable quest for truth and justice, with the world.

Marianne Williamson's idea of a US Department of Children and Youth is a noble step towards giving due attention to issues concerning children, including education.

As a quick side note, if you want to take your company or organisation to the next level, consider employing a person on the autism spectrum for a fresh perspective and potentially ground-breaking new solutions to your work. It can really up-level your game. *Fortune favours the bold*, as they say.

Dr Tracie O'Keefe DCH, BHSc, ND, is a clinical hypnotherapist, psychotherapist, and counsellor with over 25 years of experience in full-time clinical practice. As a life-long learner and teacher, I asked Tracie about her thoughts on education:

"Education serves many purposes for an individual and within a society including helping a person move through their life successfully, creating skills to enable them to make a living, exist in social harmony, and encouraging creativity and personal achievement.

"Many educational institutions, however, generally produce students who will fit into the industrial machine to create commercial profits and wealth. Students are pushed into pass or fail situations which misses a large degree of their human talent and unique abilities. This ends up creating individuals who lead highly stressed and unsatisfied lives with feelings of unworthiness, constantly striving to do or be 'enough', as we can see from ever-increasing levels of anxiety, depression and mental illness.

"Finland does things differently. The country ranks at the top of almost every educational standard. There are small classes of variable ages, with highly trained teachers and diverse subjects of students' choosing. Children spend less time at school with hardly any homework and are frequently multi-lingual. So the students' level of enjoyment and engagement is much higher. A constant sense of positive encouragement from teachers produces happy, well-educated students.

"This is typically how I like to teach hypnotherapy students in my masterclasses. Small-group work allows the students to get a high level of individual attention, to ask questions, and to become better hypnotherapists. I use a lot of practical, experiential teaching so the students retain their knowledge for life, rather than simply learning something by rote to pass an exam, then forgetting the material.

"Positive education is based on students having had a high level of pleasure and enjoyment from the learning process. They look forward to studying, developing their knowledge, intellect, and analytical skills and sharing those with others. This contributes to happy, healthy, and compassionate societies."

Science and technology

The production and distribution of this book would not have been possible without science and technology. Computers, the Internet, email, online book stores, mobile phones, publishing software, and printers were all part of creating the book you are either reading on an electronic device or in printed form. Humans are a clever bunch.

Scientific advances are exciting because of the potential for good they bring to the world, and scary because of their potential for bad.

I'm the type of person who relishes focusing on the positive possibilities and doesn't like to look at what is broken in the world, seeking to manifest what could be instead of what is. But, in order to get there, to positive-land, an acknowledgement of the current state of play is needed. As you read through the current stuff, stay strong and know that there are tons of positive solutions and inspiring examples in the book, and that this book is solutions orientated, not a doom and gloom saga. Okay, let's get started.

Whether you regard the existence of the continent known as Atlantis as a myth or not, it is a cautionary tale, nonetheless. In Atlantis, Centaurs (half people, half animals) were the result of humans thinking they could alter themselves physically to a drastic extent. Nature wasn't perfect enough for them and their technological ability surpassed their ethics to such a degree that they rendered themselves obsolete.

Meanwhile, on Earth in the present time, humans are racing ahead, developing technology with little consideration of the consequences as a whole and with minimal ethical consideration. Now we are seeing reports of animal and human tissue being combined as monkey-human chimeras. These kinds of experiments aim to further scientific advancement for medical purposes, but in the wrong hands the results could be even more disastrous than they already are. It goes without saying that these experiments are unethical, cruel to animals, and totally unnecessary.

Ray Kurzweil is a long-time futurist and a director of engineering at Google. Kurzweil predicts that nanotechnology implants will render our bodies part human, part robot. Indeed, this has somewhat begun with people microchipping themselves, so far in the name of convenience. This technology may be seen by some as being beneficial but, it needs to be critically reviewed at all stages to ensure it doesn't go from voluntary to compulsory and start violating people's right to their own bodily autonomy.

There is also talk of smart dust, which is dust with cognitive programming embedded within it, that can be emitted into the atmosphere to invisibly influence at best, and interrupt and re-program at worst, human thoughts.

That's seriously next level, but consider how fast technology has developed even within the past ten years, and you can see that we need to keep one step ahead of where we are heading and think properly about how we manage technological potentials.

In *The Decline of the West*, Oswald Spengler talks about human history going in cycles rather than evolving in a straight line. He references lost civilisations that have previously reached high points in modernisation, only to collapse and begin the cycle again.

Wise policy in the area of science and technology requires a thorough understanding of all the possible consequences of rapidly accelerating 'progress', lest our civilisation becomes another Atlantis. Ethics and justice must guide our adoption and implementation of new technologies so that they are beneficial rather than harmful. We must question the true value of a supposed medical advance or security measure — especially if one small group stands to profit — if it deprives humans of their privacy and freedom, or harms other animals and our environment. Research and development teams may intend to produce treatments and programs that assist in the next phase of human evolution, but they must temper their enthusiasm with an understanding that their innovations may end up in the hands of those who are more interested in wealth, power, and control over others. As the saying goes, "The road to hell is paved with good intentions".

Here Plato describes the descent of Atlanteans:

"But when the divine portion began to fade away, and became diluted too often and too much with the mortal admixture, and the human nature got the upper hand, they then, being unable to bear their fortune, behaved unseemly, and to him who had an eye to see grew visibly debased, for they were losing the fairest of their precious gifts; but to those who had no eye to see the true happiness, they appeared glorious and blessed at the very time when they were full of avarice and unrighteous power." Plato, *Timaeus/Critias*

Sound familiar? In other words, if your eyes are open to what is really happening, you see a different picture compared to someone who contemplates little and looks only at issues superficially.

If you think it's impossible or ridiculous for the history books not to be plainly stating details of civilisations such as Atlantis and Lemuria, consider the Australian Government's reluctance to set the history records straight by renaming Australian Day as Invasion day. History gets conveniently rewritten everywhere. "Who controls the past controls the future: who controls the present controls the past." *George Orwell, 1984*

Just as it has become the case that if a person questions the number of vaccines given at once or asks any questions about vaccines, they are automatically branded an 'anti-vaxxer', so too it may be that if you question being microchipped, you will be ridiculed or ostracised as an 'anti-microchipper'. A coercive society uses scorn and shame against those who question that coercion. Freedom to do with your own body what you will is being increasingly threatened, as governments and their agencies enforce their policies. People who refuse to vaccinate their kids, for whatever reason — right or wrong — are now refused entry to schooling, in some places within Australia.

Indeed, doctors have been de-registered not because they are anti-vaccination, but simply because they questioned the number of vaccines given at the one appointment. There are more and more symptoms of a controlling government emerging, and the more you pay attention, the more you notice. I have no interest in advocating for or against vaccines, that is a matter of science and personal choice. What is disturbing is being told that something is compulsory and that we don't have control over what we allow into our own bodies. Our right to bodily autonomy is being slowly eroded. Lastly, as a slight (but very important) aside, testing vaccines designed for humans on animals is cruel, unjust, ineffective and inefficient.

But, none of this super gloomy stuff needs to happen. It's not too late at all. Being aware and really, genuinely considering who you are voting for and what their agenda truly is, is paramount to co-creating a world where human rights and dignities are retained. If you are not satisfied with political candidate and party choices, I urge you to start your own political party, pending your country's rules. There will be others who will join you. Make history. Take a stand. We need you to get involved in the political process and display the ethical leadership humanity needs right now to go forward in a meaningful, safe and ethical direction.

Global affairs

There are certain factions who believe it would be better if there was one central government that looked after the whole world. Given the size and complexity of our global community, it is impossible to see this being an option that would meet the distinct and varying needs of different environments, population densities, and heritages. This isn't necessary nor is it desirable if ethical governments were to exist in all nations. A worldwide forum similar in function to the United Nations is helpful to discuss how to better support each other and face global issues. But, each nation should be encouraged to govern autonomously and according to their own unique, beautiful culture and traditions. The more each nation celebrates and develops their own positive aspects and the worldwide media reports such happenings, the closer the world will be in friendship and peace. As time progresses, if you hear information in the media about a one world government, analyse and question why this is necessary and who is behind such ideas. Keeping curious and alert to the world we live in ensures we don't fall for attempts by the powerful to become even more powerful. Should, at some point, there be many advantages to creating such a global government, and such a government is operated by wise, compassionate, loving souls, then this is a matter of consideration by the global human race. But, until such a time, be cautious and aware.

Finance

Ethical investing is a relatively new concept to the finance world. Claire Smith is someone at the forefront of breaking new ground in this regard. I asked Claire why she started Beyond Investing and the US Vegan Climate Exchange Traded Fund (ETF):

"I started Beyond Investing because of my own frustration as an investor in being unable to find any suitable investment vehicle that I could trust to steer clear of any animal exploitation. As a vegan myself, it was anathema to me to invest in companies engaged in activities to which I am opposed. "The need was particularly relevant from the perspective of my self-managed pension fund, since it required me to invest in fund vehicles, not stocks. The US Vegan Climate Index has been developed with my partners Lee Coates and Larry Abele to address this gap in the market. It seeks to avoid exposure to any activities involving profiting from animal exploitation, and because we care about all animals and the environment, we also screen out some damaging industries like fossil fuel, plastics, and mining companies with poor environmental and human rights records.

"The US Vegan Climate Exchange Traded Fund (ticker: VEGN) tracks the Index that we have created, and as it is listed on the New York Stock Exchange, it provides a simple, tax-efficient, and easily traded packaged investment for any investor in the US, and elsewhere, if their brokerage platform provides access to US ETFs, who wants to run their own money according to vegan and environmentally-friendly principles.

"Our expectation is that the fund will become the go-to strategy for any individual investor concerned about these issues, as well as charities and foundations whose mission is to promote animal welfare and protect the environment, and companies that explicitly adopt a vegan ethos will want to offer the option of VEGN to their employees for their pensions. Should assets grow, we will use the financial muscle that we have to engage with companies to encourage them to stop these damaging practices and to embed vegan values into all of their decision-making."

Investing involves risk, including the possible loss of principal. The index methodology may cause the Fund to underperform the broader equity market or other funds which do not utilize such criteria. The Fund's return may not match or achieve a high degree of correlation with the return of the underlying Index. To the extent the Fund utilizes a representative sampling approach, it may experience tracking error to a greater extent than if the Fund had sought to replicate the Index.

The fund's investment objectives, risks, charges and expenses must be considered carefully before investing. The prospectus contains this and other important information about the investment company, and it may be obtained by calling 1-800-617-0004 or visiting www. veganetf.com. Read it carefully before investing.

Beyond Investing LLC is the adviser to the US Vegan Climate ETF. VEGN is distributed by Quasar Distributors, LLC

Chapter Three

Options for Future Political Organisation
and How to Vote Consciously in Future Elections

This chapter lays out a few examples of different ways to reorganise the political process. The aim is to ignite ideas and further discussion about where we can go from here.

Business as usual and why it needs to change

The political party donation systems need ethical restructuring and monitoring. Each party or candidate (for independents) should be given an equal cap on donations and they use those funds to campaign and no more than that.

Political parties shouldn't be influenced by corporations and interest groups like mining, animal agriculture, or anybody else for that matter. Putting a cap on political donations will actually safeguard parties and allow them to make decisions independent of who has funded their election victory. It will also inevitably make the playing field fairer and will allow policy, intelligence and leadership capability to be at the forefront of campaigns instead of incessant advertising by the more affluent parties and candidates. This is a must for better political outcomes. Pretty much everyone knows this, it's simply a matter of legislating it. Making it happen.

As Sean Kelly, former advisor to Prime Ministers Kevin Rudd and Julia Gillard, said: "'Whatever it takes' has, over time, become our national motto. If only our leaders would apply that attitude where it is really needed: killing the corrupting influence of donations, stopping the relentless pursuit of profit over morality, and restoring the most basic level of integrity to our public life."

Philanthropists could consider directing some of their funds towards innovative and ethical political parties, in addition to their other causes. Parliaments potentially change and create laws which affect every sphere of life for all beings on Earth. It's powerful stuff. Funding ethical candidates and parties goes towards the foundation of creating an ethical society. Imagine if unconditional philanthropists funded political campaigns instead of the vested interests of corporations *and* there was a cap on donations. We may see a very different political scene and outcomes in elections.

A note on the illusion of scarcity

In the absence of real policy, fear-based campaigns are run on the economics of lack. The illusion of scarcity is peddled out every election season, scaring voters into believing that if they don't vote for their party, they will not have a job.

Scarcity, which is what economic theory is grounded in, is an absolute illusion. The entire premise of economic theory isn't real. Strange, but true. Tragic even.

You will tell me, "But look at the water and food shortages around the world. That is evidence of scarcity." I would say to that, it is simply evidence of the few having too much and the multitude being forgotten in the pursuit of greed. We have more than enough if resources are allocated fairly and justly to everyone. We need to share more than take. Try it and feel the change within yourself. If you start to believe in abundance, you will start to share a little more and notice that things get better for you and those around you. It's a nice feeling to share, even if it starts with something small. It's the universal law of cause and effect, or karma, in spiritual speak, in action. It doesn't matter if you follow the scientific explanation or the spiritual one, it's all the same and the result is an equitable distribution of resources and ultimately, world peace. If there are to be wars in the future, they will undoubtedly be about food and water. It's so unnecessary. We share. We fix the world.

The first step towards a peaceful world is adopting a peaceful diet. By reducing our carbon footprint through adopting a plant-based, vegan diet, we aid in assisting in this water and food shortage also. There's no point talking about peace when we are eating the by-products of cruelty, which is what consuming a diet comprised of animal products is. Plain and simple. *The World Peace Diet* by Will Tuttle, PhD is the go-to book on this subject.

Slogans are so last century

Elections are sadly often reduced to slogans that are framed by their opponents as being either 'anti' or 'pro' an issue. Many issues are complex and require details to be explained, but the simplicity in which they are reduced by opponents trying to score votes with their constituents, means parties with well-developed policies are shot down as being 'anti' or 'pro' something, which is not always the case. This was a point Australian Senator Penny Wong made during the 2019 Federal Election campaign, when she was on the ABC TV panel during the election results coverage.

Big, rich countries need to take responsibility

The Australian Government's reticence to assist neighbouring islands relocate because of climate change is ironic and cruel, given that Australia contributes much more towards the negative impacts of climate change than the small island nations requesting assistance. Not good enough. Love thy neighbour. It's basic. Many of the leaders of Australia claim to be Catholic or another Christian denomination but don't follow the philosophy that Jesus made deliberately simple, so there was no misunderstanding. But still. Misunderstanding? I think not. They are simply ignoring their basic duties as a neighbour. This is not the government I want to represent me.

This is pointing out the obvious and one of the reasons people tune out and get disengaged in the political system. They feel helpless and sick of it all.

This is what it *could* look like: wise, compassionate, intelligent guides of countries. No dominating over others. No egotistical, self-serving decisions.

Political leadership has become a bad joke that never ends. It doesn't have to stay that way. Some politicians are alright, not too harmful. But we need more than alright to get humanity out of the mess it's in. And we need it... yesterday. Climate change, climate refugees, political refugees, food and water shortages, etc. We need seriously courageous, intelligent leaders who aren't afraid to get stuff done to solve these big issues.

I've spoken to high ranking parliamentary representatives who've said they would love to put forward more progressive policies, but the current mentality of the voters is such that it would mean they wouldn't be voted in. So we can complain about bad politicians but we can also look at the consciousness of the people and what they are interested in voting for. We get what we deserve. If we want better, we must be better, and then we can elect better. The same goes for business. Major fast food chains are all-of-a-sudden producing and selling vegan burgers. Have they had a sudden crisis of conscience? Mostly, no. They recognise the growing demand for plant-based food and are simply meeting the market where it's at.

Some politicians are really sincere people who go into politics as a way of public service. They have high ideals and high hopes, but get caught up in the 'machine' of major party politics. The emergence of micro parties brings hope that the two party system will become less and less relevant as every election comes around. Some people are voting on single issues that matter to them through these micro parties.

Governments need to look beyond their one term: help farmers transition to plant based industries and further develop renewable energy; the powerful solutions to climate change and other environmental issues. People need jobs. Coal and animal agriculture aren't sustainable industries and we don't need to cling to them and support them for economic or environmental reasons. Change is scary but can also be awesome and profitable. And planet saving. You know. The seriously important stuff.

Beyond party politics

Instead of fighting over who should run the government every three to four years and spending incredible amounts of money on campaigns, perhaps the installation of a wise, ethical council to oversee bureaucratic functions such as administering hospitals, public transport, and other social services could be one of many alternative options. This would only work once human society has evolved to a certain extent, and is ready and happy for such an alternative. It would enable more funds to go towards public services without paying for elections and many other associated costs.

Popularly electing representatives under the parliamentary democratic system doesn't necessarily produce the best outcomes for a society. If you disagree, look at what we have currently manifested with this system. Popularity contests can at times produce good leaders. This is certainly not a pitch for dictatorships nor communism. It's simply a recognition that in a peaceful society where citizens prize ethics, governments would reflect this and would be run accordingly.

True democracy is an amazing way to enable the expression of the will of the people. Parliamentary democracy isn't real democracy because voters only get to choose whoever the parties put forward as their candidates. When you vote, you think you're choosing. Not true. You're choosing from a narrow list of pre-chosen candidates. That's why people get so disillusioned because they realise, they really aren't getting leaders that represent them at all. For those countries that *are* more democratic in nature, problems still exist because of uncapped donations and the more financially supported candidates consequently having the campaign advantage.

And, once these people are voted in, they need to tow party lines, so there's actually a lot of power among a small number of people who are calling the shots from behind the scenes. It happens here in Australia and in many other countries.

There are various solutions to this. One of the most peace-promoting, positive solutions is for more ethical, harmonious people to enter the political sphere. At the same time the general consciousness and compassion of the voters needs to elevate, as they realise that it's in everyone's best interests to do the right thing and care for each other, animals, and nature/environment.

Indigenous wisdom and healing the Earth

Colonialism has created environmental disaster. There's no point being polite about it, it is what it is. People arrive in foreign lands and exploit them without knowledge or care for the original inhabitants, including Indigenous peoples, animals and the natural landscape.

The time is now to listen to the Indigenous peoples of all lands and learn from them about how to erase the damage that's been done. All governments must include Indigenous elders in the conversation about environmental protection and healing the land.

Decolonising food and getting back to nature is a very important issue for many cultures. Writers and activists from numerous African nations have written articles about decolonising food and getting back to their traditional, largely plant-based diets.

More respect and serious attention needs to be given to Indigenous activists who have marked sensitivity and understanding about natural resources. The great work that Autumn Peltier is doing, for example, for water protection from childhood needs more media and government attention and action. Children shouldn't need to give up their childhoods to do the work that adults won't do.

Aunty Ro Mudyin Godwin is an Indigenous activist in Australia with a deep understanding of environmental issues and a passion for speaking the truth at all costs. Aunty Ro has kindly allowed me to reprint the following extract of a post she wrote on Facebook in the midst of the 2019/2020 summer bushfire disaster that swept through the East coast of Australia, resulting in more than a billion animals being killed.

"Land clearing is at the core of colonialism as is genocide and is a very real and ongoing problem which is still completely ignored!

"It's at the heart of the unsustainable farming sector: logging, obviously, and ditto mining. These are all introduced to Country. They were never here before settlement. Country was never abused with relentless greedy take and the fires you see before you are a message about that greedy take needing to stop, but it's still being ignored!

"To keep it simple, land clearing across vast tracts destroys Country. It results in the die back of any Indigenous vegetation that remains. It cooks the soils and destroys the microbes in soil which are essential for germination and soil health. It also releases greenhouse gas emissions and changes rainfall patterns by altering the circulation of heat and moisture and by increasing the surface temperatures.

"Then on top of that you add 72 million head of sheep and 26 million head of cattle. None of these exploited animals are suited to Country. They are hard hoofed, water dependent, root grazing animals. Then, on top of that you add the systematic eradication of wildlife: flying foxes, wombats, cockatoos and especially kangaroos. All of our wildlife play an essential role in the biodiversity of Country. They all form links in a very intricate chain that has seen Country not only sustain we Indigenous people for 60,000 years but sustain plentiful wildlife and indeed itself for millions of years; and now, look around: Country is dying and it's being *encouraged*!

"Song Lines and Dreaming Tracks are dying. The very interconnectedness of Country is dying and it's all because of this continuing disconnected greedy take!

"To systematically eradicate the very wildlife who play an essential role in the regeneration of Country and in its very survival is completely counterproductive.

"Kangaroos are regenerators of the bush, always have been. Kangaroos aerate soils as they move around with the large toenail at the front of their feet and the structure of the forearm claws moving soils as they themselves indeed move. This causes aeration of soils and undergrowth which is also essential in overall soil health and regeneration. Kangaroos eat soil, bark, dry foliage, sticks etc., thus again, naturally reducing the level of undergrowth on Country by eating seeds and having that seed excreted in a neat package of nutrient dense kanga poo. They also aid in seed dispersal just by top grazing. They again aid in seed dispersal that of course then aids in an increased plant growth thus reducing surface temperatures. And the same regarding kanga poo: it's the most naturally nutrient dense vitamin package around and brilliant for aiding plant growth, yet those with all of their 231 years of colonial knowledge have labelled kangaroos as a pest to be eradicated.

Oh, the irony of the 'introduced pests' labelling kangaroos as a pest!

"Increased land clearing, increased slaughter of wildlife, especially kangaroos, means there's no way for Country to naturally regenerate itself. Then there's the destruction of Song Lines and Dreaming Tracks and people are wondering *why* we are seeing the bushfire intensity we are seeing right now? *Seriously?*

"Now you can slash, cut grass, even cartwheel naked down the street if you like, but nothing is going to stop these bushfires increasing in intensity if the core of the problem isn't addressed.

"Climate change is a very real problem and it has land clearing as its predominant cause. This must be addressed and action taken to stop it. I'm not talking about token gestures: "Oh we must reduce this or that". That opportunity has been and gone. Now it must stop and with capitalism at the core of the unsustainable farming sector and at the core of government, how that happens will be very interesting to watch.

"This lunacy of slaughtering wildlife must stop. And where are all the other Indigenous people who always rant on about culture in all this? Why am I the only Black Fella standing up as the lone fearless Indigenous woman saying enough *is* enough?!

"These are the main problems that are continuing to be ignored, especially the slaughter of Kangaroos. How ignorant would you have to be to legislate the systematic slaughter of Kangaroos when it's they who *naturally* reduce bushfire intensity and risk *and* how the hell is Country going to regenerate and recover from these fires when the very animals essential in the regeneration process have been gunned down by the very unsustainable farming sector and governments who are the instigators of all this carnage?!

"As I've said over and over and over again, these fires are the rage of those slain in 232 years of settlement of Country. Millions of kangaroos slaughtered. Indigenous peoples slaughtered. Wildlife *en masse* slaughtered all due to colonialism fuelled greed and disconnect. Country damned to death. Rivers drained. And people wonder why we are seeing the rage of these fires? *Really?* You think the abuse and greedy take that has happened for 232 years can continue with no consequences? *Seriously?*

"These fires are a reminder of what happens when warnings are continuously ignored. How many droughts do you people have to put yourselves through before the penny drops? How many bushfires will it take for people to understand the enormity of the situation they continue to ignore? How much longer are you going to let a minority function in such a way that it destroys the majority?

"How much longer will *you* remain ignorant and finger point at others whilst refusing to see where the real problem lies?

"And make no mistake if people don't wake up soon and very quickly to what is being created and indeed, ignored, then these fires now will be nothing compared to what Ancestors will hit us with in the future."

What you can do: a guide for voters

Vote, vote, vote

If you live in a country where voting is optional, please do vote. Every vote counts. Your input can change the outcome for the better. Elections can be decided by one vote. Your opinion matters. Please make it count. And on that note, take the time to ensure you understand how a vote is counted. For example, if your country has specific rules about how many boxes you need to number in order for your vote to count, please take care to get it right. Don't be afraid or embarrassed to ask someone if you need help or clarification.*

If you consider yourself as 'not being into politics', then your complacency and indifference becomes what we have today: leaders who don't care about serving nations properly, because they know very well that the voters are disengaged, won't protest, don't care...until their consistent indifference culminates in a crisis. Don't blame the leaders, it's a collective effort, a build up of energy that results in the leaders you deserve. Harsh, but truth is never easy to digest. Obviously this is not for people who vote consciously and honestly try to do what they can. And yes, there are not always inspiring choices *but if you give up, we have no chance.*

* *If it's safe in your country to do so. This comment is really for democratic, relatively stable countries where voting is optional. In the future, as people evolve spiritually, peaceful elections will be the norm throughout the planet. Until then, take care.*

I fully recognise how hard it can be to decipher political campaign promises and work out who to vote for, and I fully acknowledge my privilege of education both academic and experiential. It's not nice to shame people who voted for a party that turns out to be rotten, if that voter did so in good faith and honestly thought that candidate or party would have the best interests of the nation at heart, even if to other people it was obvious that was not the case. I can't bear intellectual and academic snobbery and putting people down because they aren't educated enough or have enough time to do the research. This is certainly not a book that aims to incite shame on any level. This book is a friend who wants to acknowledge how hard it can be to make a good choice when it seems like it's impossible because of the 'no choice' choice.

To conclude, I fully acknowledge corrupt elements within governments both here in Australia and overseas, but focusing on it and wasting pages commentating on it won't really get us far. It goes deep, far, and wide. You can find information about it if you search. We must get ethical people into politics and fast so that voting can be a straight forward exercise due to ethical political candidates and parties being transparent and honest during their campaigns. No second guessing required.

Practice active thinking

Stay informed. Look behind the headlines. Question everything. Be an actively thinking person not a passive consumer of information. Proactively seek out information about candidates beyond the mainstream media outlets, who often have narrow agendas and preferences. Look for bias. It's all over the front covers of newspapers. Being an active thinker will keep you engaged in the truth and will avoid passive acceptance of unacceptable and subpar candidates and policies.

The incumbent advantage

Don't let the fact that the present government has the power deter you from applying for their positions. The world needs fresh ideas, more positive approaches and most of all, courageous and ethical leaders who are unafraid of doing what needs to be done, with a sense of urgency and awareness. We need that right now and will it need going forward to sort everything out.

The children who are striking about climate change, led by Greta Thunberg will be voting in a couple of years. They will then start infiltrating as leaders on all levels. It's just a natural process. These higher consciousness souls are all over the planet. It means the global political game will change for the better. Thank goodness.

Single and limited issue parties: proceed with caution

Micro and single issue parties that have begun to spring up are great for alerting the public to issues that have not been adequately covered by the major parties, such as animal protection and the environment. However, the importance of these parties having a position statement on *all* major policies cannot be understated. Why? Because, if elected, these candidates get to vote on *everything*, not just their topics of interest. It's very important that voters don't assume that these parties are in alignment with their values just because they align with one or five or even ten of their values.

Also, the lack of experience of the new single issue parties needs to be balanced by deep consideration of where they stand on everything they could be potentially voting on in parliament, and making those positions known to the public before elections. It's only fair.

Single issue, limited issue, and micro parties: if you broaden your knowledge in anticipation for voting on all issues, you will also get more respect from the bigger parties and will be treated more seriously in negotiations for your issues and platforms. Whether you regard your political party as single issue or not, the way the public and your fellow parliamentary members perceive it, is what ultimately matters in terms of votes and how your colleagues from other parties regard you.

It also gives voters enhanced confidence in voting for these parties, as it illustrates that these parties are capable of seeing the bigger picture. It can result in more votes and more representation for that party in parliament. Micro parties argue that they have no intention of governing a nation, they just want their special interest to be represented in parliament, and/or gain the potential balance of power. This is fine, but this is not how the majority of voters see the situation. They want to see their local representative pay attention and be knowledgeable in the macro economic issues as well.

It illustrates the ability to see cause and effect of policy implementation and present as a well-rounded representative. What *you* want to do in parliament is not as important as how *voters* make voting decisions. It's the same as you loving the product you sell isn't as important as your potential customers understanding what the benefit of the product could be for them if they buy it. You need to sell your capability as a political party and a candidate as much as a fruit seller sells the benefits of eating fruit. It's all selling in the end, and the "What's in it for me?" line is as relevant in politics as it is in selling goods and services.

A small party will be unstoppable in terms of success if they present themselves as knowledgeable and across all policy portfolios. They will be able to eliminate any potential voter objections and truly stand out from the crowd.

Looking beyond rhetoric

Rhetoric, according to the Oxford English Dictionary, is, "Language designed to have a persuasive or impressive effect, but which is often regarded as lacking in sincerity or meaningful content."

The ability to look beyond rhetoric is a skill that should be taught in school. Slogans are just that. Look beyond the talk and see what substance and evidence there is that the candidate or party you are considering voting for (depending on your country's system) will do what they say they will do, or whether they have the capacity to develop a full policy based on their slogans. 'Jobs and growth', a commonly used slogan among certain political parties in Australia means very little to me. Don't fall for it. What is the substance behind it? If there is none then you are voting based on rhetoric alone. A very dicey choice at best, disastrous at worst. If you vote based on pure rhetoric without doing a little bit of research at the very least, you risk falling for what the major parties predict you will: taking their word for it and trusting they will follow through with their promises.

Peaceful pollies

Strive for peace in all transactions and interactions with others. Look for commonalities between people instead of the differences. Inside we are all one, all brothers and sisters. Parliamentary debating is too savage. Be graceful, respectful, courteous to others. You are our elected representatives. Where are your dignity and manners? Be the example of great leaders we can look up to, be inspired to vote for and engage with in the political process. Leave a legacy. Dare to be different and stand out, in a good way.

This is partly a thinking book but it is also equal parts a being book. How are you being? What kind of presence do you have with others? Do you radiate conflict more so than peace? How's that working out for you? Our knowledge will only take us so far. When you combine knowledge with a peaceful disposition, you become a truly powerful force for positive, sustainable progress for humanity, animals, and the planet.

Working on polishing and refining our energy first and foremost is essential for sustainable peace and successfully implementing positive solutions for the planet. Otherwise, it's just empty words and all too theoretical. If we talk about peace we need to be peaceful inside.

Assumptions for a Golden Age way of living

In a Golden Age world, citizens value the well-being of their fellow citizens as much as they value their own. Nobody takes what is not theirs to take. Nobody harms other living beings. Violence is seen as counterproductive to the greater good of the peace and harmony of a nation, because it upsets the balance of nature.

In such a world, people are sensitive and in tune with nature and themselves. They cultivate their own wisdom and virtues through spiritual practice. They realise that all actions come from thoughts and that a pure mind of good intentions is the cornerstone of a happy life for themselves and those around them. They realise that ego is the destroyer of all things and humility is prized as something to aspire to from childhood. In school, virtue is taught as much as other subjects. Ethical living is part of the core curriculum.

We need to implement the advice from climate scientists. Do every single thing we can to assist the Earth to heal herself. Listen to the Indigenous people of all nations for they are deeply connected to Mother Earth. And, do everything we can to learn from our mistakes. Humans should never dominate the planet ever again.

May peace reign on Earth once more...

Chapter 4

When the Feminine Guides the World: Uniting Nations Through the Leadership of Vegan Women

Will Tuttle, author of the best-selling book *The World Peace Diet* wrote the foreword to my first book, *Forever 21*. I've never forgotten his words of support for feminine power. He wrote, "Sophia, our long-repressed inner feminine wisdom, is rising in our collective consciousness, and as she does, we are remembering ancient truths about our interconnectedness with all life, and our purpose on this Earth…Sophia is irrepressible, and rises up in us as the sacred sense of caring for this Earth and for all life, manifesting as our saying yes to the benevolent inclusiveness of veganism, and saying no to the cultural expectations of eating and using animals as mere instruments for our questionable benefit."

Humanity is at a crucial moment in its story where it will either rise to the occasion and intelligently, wisely, and compassionately address urgent global concerns or it will continue like business-as-usual, and follow the known and ineffective path.

If we desire different outcomes, we need to initiate different solutions. One solution is to graciously and respectfully hand over the leadership to women and others who are connected to their inner feminine wisdom, so we may enter into an era of gentle guidance; to finally achieve world peace for all beings on Earth.

Why should women lead the world?

Imagine a world of true collaboration. There are so many women capable of working together to do what needs to be done to bring Earth and our human existence back into balance. We have an urgent need to bring together women with a gentle, nurturing nature who can put forth intelligent, workable solutions to heal and repair this turbulent world. This book serves as a big call out to women everywhere to step into leadership positions within your community to start the process of healing and repairs. Enough with all of the wars and conflicts and the plethora of ego-driven nonsense. A peace driven change is long overdue. Ethical leadership is long overdue.

What is ethical leadership?

Ethical leadership is about genuinely caring for people, animals and the planet. It's about everyday conscious action. It's a vegan life and a peaceful life.

Why vegan women?

Vegan women have made the conscious decision to live a life of compassion and consideration for all beings. They are ethically fit to lead and have this moral baseline from which to act that makes them great leadership candidates. In this book you have already heard from several vegan women such as Katrina Fox, Clare Mann, and Jenny McCracken, among others who are part of the movement of positive, ethical change within their communities. It is this kind of leadership that we need to see more of in order to bring about the depth of change needed to correct the problems on this planet. There are many great examples all over the planet. Greta Thunberg is one who has made a big impact in recent times for her simple message of urgent action on the climate crisis.

Vegan women speak

The following are messages from vegan women. Some speak of peace, others offer advice to aspiring leaders and the remainder talk about the work they are doing to make the world a fairer, kinder place for all beings. The other quotes from women featured in this book in the earlier chapters also form part of this illustration of the talents and leadership abilities of vegan women.

Dr Tamasin Ramsay
Research and Policy Advisor, for Mr Andy Meddick, MLC
(Western Victoria), Animal Justice Party

People who are vegan, and who are so because of a deep and abiding sense of justice, often move away from politics. I understand why. In Australia we live on land that was stolen, and within a political system that is embedded in the crimes of colonisation. We can't go back. But we can move ahead. And women are the key.

I believe women can do anything. I believe this because I have witnessed it every day for most of my life. I was brought up by a woman who had nothing and yet created a safe and abundant world for me. I have been travelling to India since the 1980s where my mentors were elderly women who lived through the most harrowing of times; their greatest power was kindness. I have represented an NGO at the United Nations whose main representatives were all women and I have noticed, through their listening and collaborating, how feminine leadership can change conversations. I then became part of the animal liberation and protection movement where most of the work is done by women. Women, especially women who are vegan because of a deep and abiding sense of justice, hold the immense power of fierce compassion. It doesn't matter who you are or where you come from. I failed high school and got myself a PhD. I was an apolitical dedicated sister in a meditation order
and am now Parliamentary Adviser to an MP for the Animal Justice Party. I had no plan, no strategy, no overarching vision. But I did have a drive, a sense of urgency, and training in compassion.

The secret to vegan women being successful (success — fulfilment and flourishing) in the political world is not the right degree, the right marketing, or the right suit. It is the power of fierce compassion, faith in feminine leadership, and a willingness to get dressed and turn up.

Use the power of your compassion ferociously — create, articulate and persevere in your own individual way. Be bold enough to take supports from others. Be insightful enough to offer to yourself the deepest respect. Be resolutely kind in all situations without exception. Train yourself. Do whatever it takes. Compassion is the force, and kindness is the power that the world needs, and that ultimately nothing can resist. They are inclusive, never exclusive. They welcome, never marginalise. They integrate, never separate.

Dr Aryan Tavakkoli MRCP FRACP CFMP
Medical Director, Quantum Clinic, UK

Scientists have long been advising a wide scale change in our lifestyles and dietary habits for planetary health. Eating plants, rather than animals, is far better for our health, and our environment. The facts are out there, and have been for some time. Knowing the facts, however, isn't enough to create change, otherwise, in this time of escalating chronic disease and environmental turbulence, the whole world would be plant-based. The question is no longer why, but how?

Addressing the critical state of both our health and our climate requires a radical shift in our behaviour towards plant-based eating. But that shift requires a change in lifelong habits, a challenging task. Change, however, must come about — our planetary crisis dictates it.

Perhaps the answer is to re-connect with our human-ness.

There is a quality that every one of us possesses, that has the power to change our thoughts and actions much more quickly than the knowledge of cold facts alone.

It's simple.

Kindness.

The mark of a human being, and overwhelming in its power, kindness can irrevocably change the lives of those it touches and will leave its imprint on this Earth long after we have left, shaping the lives of those to come.

Once we re-connect with that innate quality, no longer will it be humanly possible for us to accept any act of cruelty, direct or indirect. The shedding of blood for 'food' will be perceived as an abhorrent, unnecessary act. We will respect the lives of all species and will naturally prefer to consume plants.

By no longer partaking in the merciless abuse of animals for food, we will simply and naturally move towards plant-based eating, and thus, almost effortlessly support the wellbeing of the environment and our own health.

Whilst governing bodies play a vital role in creating change, we don't have to be a politician to create significant changes. The power lies within our hands at this very moment.

"Yesterday I was clever so I wanted to change the world. Today I am wise so I am changing myself." Rumi

By allowing our daily decisions to be governed by kindness, we will change the path of humankind towards greater happiness, harmony and abundance in every way.

The change we need now is achievable, and kindness is the key.

Palak Mehta
Founder and CEO, Vegan First, India
Vice Chair - World Vegan Organisation - India Chapter

I was raised as a non-vegetarian, which is the case with most Punjabi families. However, I realised that I had a choice to choose my diet when I was in grade 10 at school. I quit meat briefly at the time, but couldn't sustain it. A couple of years later, I even started on a high energy raw vegan diet but, like a passing trend, quit that too.

During my college years, I met my spiritual Master, Mohanji. His teachings of compassion, unity and peace resonated with me deeply. After meeting him, I started thinking beyond me and myself. Over the years I've seen animals walk up to him, and bask in the loving energy He radiates. I've seen several animals get healed by Him. On one occasion, in Dharamshala there were dogs fighting with each other, and Mohanji was actually translating their communication and feelings to some of us present there. Mohanji has always considered them as equal beings to humans who have feelings and emotions and who also deserve an equal amount of respect. I always felt for the environment and animals but never felt empowered enough to do something about it. My interest and participating in adding value to Earth grew and was nurtured by Mohanji always.

Around 2011 I was exposed to the animal cruelty in our food and lifestyle through Mohanji's teachings. He started talking about veganism and sharing videos of the horrendous practices at dairy farms, hatcheries and slaughterhouses. I was in disbelief and deeply hurt, I would cry for days. I was a vegetarian at the time but once I saw the reality behind dairy, I couldn't unsee it and went completely vegan. Finding vegan alternatives and information was tougher in India around five years back, so I decided to start a platform for all things vegan in India, www.veganfirst.com. I took Mohanji's blessings, and bootstrapped my way through the initial years. He even suggested the name 'Vegan First'. Today, Vegan First is India's largest vegan publication and solution space and also hosted India's first international vegan conference with participants from more than 25 countries coming together.

Billie Dean
Author and Creative, Animal Sanctuary co-founder
Billie Dean Deep Peace Trust, Australia

At the Deep Peace Trust, we look at two levels of peace.

The first is freedom from fear and a state of contentment and serenity, which every being on Earth deserves, and which we offer to every resident of our animal sanctuary.

The second is the transcendent, blissful state of deep peace.

People who reach this very high frequency state often produce artistic creations which can spark their audiences to touch higher levels of consciousness. When the resonance of deep peace ripples out into the world, it creates change. Even the words 'deep peace' create a ripple when spoken with feeling.

Transcendent peace is a state of being that most people don't yet enjoy, being immersed in fear, shame, guilt, grief, struggle, survival and other low-frequency states. But when one person breaks through to that high state, it helps others evolve through morphogenic resonance. So one of the things we do at the Trust is offer art projects and spiritual teachings, which help people work towards the personal alchemy and healing needed to produce the bliss of transcendent peace.

Imagine a world where every single soul of all species resonated deep peace. That's an evolutionary shift. And that's our vision and mission.

Victoria Moran
Author, Film Producer and Director of Main Street Vegan Academy
USA

When I came upon veganism in my twenties, I was profoundly influenced by American Vegan Society founder Jay Dinshah's book, *Out of the Jungle*. In it, he speculated that veganism was no mere philosophical doctrine: it was nonviolence playing out in real life and real time. It was peace on earth, goodwill to everybody.

My initial interest came from concern for the animals trapped in an ignominious industry. Improvements in my health convinced me that health vegans are cool too. I learned about world hunger, and found that veganism amplified my ability to live the spiritual principles I'd gleaned from a Christian upbringing, influenced by the discovery of yoga at seventeen. Long before I'd heard of climate change, this was the right way to live and eat. Today, it is the only rational way to live and eat.

I turned a college fellowship into an opportunity to study vegans in the UK, meeting movement pioneers and writing my first book, *Compassion the Ultimate Ethic*. Titles followed including *The Love-Powered Diet, The Good Karma Diet,* and *Main Street Vegan,* which spawned the Main Street Vegan Podcast; Main Street Vegan Academy, a weeklong intensive in New York City training Vegan Lifestyle Coaches and Educators: and Main Street Vegan Productions, whose first documentary is *A Prayer for Compassion*, seeking to interest people of faith in vegan living.

I believe that every vegan has a daily calling to carry this message. How we do this depends upon who we are, and what talents and resources we have, but each of us can do something no one else can. And if we do it, our children will have a future and our world will take a great evolutionary leap — "out of the jungle" and into the light.

Cassy Judy
Criminal Lawyer and Musician
Australia

Our criminal legal system emphasises individual responsibility. However, the law seems to apply more to those who are disadvantaged and the types of crimes that they commit. If one's life path is highly influenced by the postcode into which we are born, then when and how does society take responsibility for redressing this?

Criminal law courts are very real places. Often the likely result will depend on the length of someone's criminal history. If someone has received all the different types of sentences, no conviction, bonds, community service, suspended sentences (now abolished), then jail is the only possibility left. Nothing else has worked to stop re-offending. But what if a whole number of individuals face similar situations? Born into intergenerational unemployment. Attending a school with low expectations of learning.

Criminal courts hold individuals responsible for their actions. Individual responsibility is important and transformative. But when does society take responsibility?

For the fact that the postcode we are born into will have a huge impact on the kind of life that we live. For the disparities in wealth created by the economic reforms of the 80s and 90s. For an education system that gives millions of dollars to wealthy schools in the name of 'choice.' For neighbourhoods that are considered 'dangerous' and 'not nice places to live.'

And what about the people who grow up there? Are they the butt of jokes, fodder for the rest of us who had better life opportunities? Some individuals will break out of such cycles. They are the exception that proves the rule. The pattern remains the same. The criminal justice system keeps its repeat offenders coming back. And once they've gone to jail, they are more likely to return. Time and time again, they tell me, *there's no help for me in jail.*

Some people reach a turning point after having a child, or around the age of 40. If society and our political system took more responsibility for addressing systemic disadvantage, they might get there sooner. Saving us the cost of prisons and allowing them a happier, more fulfilling life sooner.

Something to consider.

Penny Rowe
Writer, Editor
Australia

As a single mother of a small child, I am a strong advocate for societal change, because my little family has so much to gain from a return to a more communal, equitable and egalitarian way of living, and I want my daughter's world to nurture her physical, emotional, social, and spiritual health.

I am passionate about whole foods, plant-based nutrition, animal rights, ecology, small-group socialism, and gentle parenting, and have long dreamed of forming an intentional community for vegan mothers and their families.

In my imagined community there would be private spaces (I am an introvert after all), as well as communal space for activities like sharing meals, creating art, dancing, and meetings both formal and informal. The emphasis would be on diverse activities both indoors and out, whilst being respectful of our internal and external environments. Food would be sourced from wildcrafted plants, our own veganic horticulture, and sensitively stocked retailers.

My goal would be to engage with others and our wider world in a healing, supportive way, rather than to isolate away from the greater challenges that our planet faces. Our children would grow up learning that what we have we share with our community, and that we care about and cherish all the people we live with, whether they are in the next room or on the other side of the globe.

Lorraine Palmer
Author and Plant-Based Food Chef
U.K.

"More Raw Is Better Than No Raw." This is what I say to women who ask for my help in banishing their symptoms brought on by the menopause. I'm talking about raw plant-based foods, it's the original fast food — pick it, blend it, chop it and eat it!

It's not necessary to eat raw plant-based foods one hundred per cent of the time to reap the health benefits from them, but by not incorporating these ingredients into your daily intake, it can cause havoc with your digestion, absorption and elimination processes. They provide hydration, roughage, and dense nutrition amongst other qualities.

I got introduced to raw plant based foods purely by accident when I was looking for ways to curb my menopause symptoms. Ingesting these foods whether it was 'Plain Ole Raw or Gourmet Raw' supported my endocrine system, and my hot flushes (flashes), crawling skin, and moodiness went away. It made sense that my symptoms would gradually subside because I was eating foods that were in their natural state — they did not spike my hormones and send them into a frenzy. I just didn't make the connection before — have you?

I'm all for the supermarkets offering processed vegan food options but there has to be a balance with what we all choose to eat, if good health and wellbeing is the aim. It's not all about over processed, sugary, highly addictive junk foods. Vegan it may be, but don't overload your body with substances it does not recognise.

I'm not a party pooper but trust me when I say, you will find it challenging to poop if *raw* plant based foods are not part of your arsenal. Toxins need to come out to ensure your body is given the best chance to serve *you* well. You have been told!

Betska K-Burr
Author, Accredited Master Coach, Trainer
Canada

Content warning: brief mention of abuse in first paragraph

After nearly four decades of emotional and sexual abuse, my mind, body and spirit shut down at the age of 38. My brain felt fuzzy, my emotions were on a continuous roller coaster ride and the pain in my lower back was so debilitating that rising up out of a chair was difficult. At that stage I was a successful executive, married to a wonderful man and our daughter was delightful. We had a beautiful home, fancy car and clothes. So why would someone who seemed to have it all shut down?

After many visits to our family doctor and natural health practitioners nothing was helping to lift me out of a depression that felt like the dark night of my soul. So what was it then? By the Grace of God, my first spiritual teacher Jan Sweeney taught me something so precious and rare that it shook me up and put me on the road to recovery. Since the subconscious mind is the driver of our lives, we absolutely must know what our subconscious beliefs are. Clearly I was ignorant to mine.

Using Jan's tools, the beliefs I discovered in my subconscious mind still blow my mind to this day! I was sooooooooooooo very negative inside while appearing to be positive on the outside. I had suppressed love. Truly I did not know how to love myself and others. I felt caged. I was numb inside. Peace eluded me.

After 3.5 months, my back pain disappeared permanently, my depression lifted and my fuzzy brain became a thing of the past. From that "awakening", I started to develop and teach globally more "tools" which we call Mind-Kinetics®. A new on-line program called "Women Rise & L.E.A.D." is designed to uplift women to "Take the L.E.A.D. & Shine"! Shine we must because the nurturing feminine is needed to help this planet heal.

Jan made it very clear to me that I needed to heal my own wounds first and open my heart and mind to become a strong leader. When I met my next spiritual teacher, Master Ching Hai, I was ready to become vegan, meditate daily and practice noble living.

Chapter 5

Preparing to be a Golden Age Leader

I *was brought up in the tradition of Confucius. It has informed my personal growth throughout my life. Confucius taught that, "To put the world in order, we must first put the nation in order; to put the nation in order, we must put the family in order; to put the family in order, we must cultivate our personal life; and to cultivate our personal life, we must first set our hearts right."*

These words are as true today as ever.

Here at the United Nations we deal with issues of global scope. To many eyes they may seem too huge to resolve.

But any problem can be broken down into small steps and individual actions.

Any problem can be solved when the heart is set right.

Ban Ki Moon – United Nations 04 September 2012

∞   ∞   ∞

In this chapter, various topics and concepts are touched upon with the aim of helping you prepare to become a leader.

Prepare yourself. Inside and out. Get ready. You're the leaders we've been waiting for.

Being a great leader

This is the era for brutal facts and truths. If we want to be a truly great planet with great nations, we need to face the truths and sincerely listen to all parties and create workable, sustainable solutions together. It's a fantastic opportunity to manifest amazing results in all aspects of life.

As you lead organisations, teams, groups or companies through the change process, you need to have absolute faith in what you are doing and why you are doing it. Sharon Pearson, author of *Disruptive Leadership* summed it up well when she said:

"You, as a leader, must stay the course. Keep talking about the new idea and keep it front of mind...Above all, persist. All new ideas go through stages of rejection to acceptance, until they are the norm, and completely integrated into what becomes the new status quo."
(Sharon Pearson, Disruptive Leadership, pg 209, reprinted with permission.)

Inner peace creates powerful leaders

In politics and in life, people often argue endlessly about who is right and who is wrong. Which country did what against which other country, or which political party is the best and which is the worst. If only we could realise that there's no time for this ongoing, incessant blame game and that the fastest, most sustainable solution is to forgive and make peace. Make peace within and without. Heal your personal wounds, send out forgiveness to your supposed enemies and then project this forgiveness and love into the bigger picture. We don't have time for anything less than that. For the sake of the next generation, be that generation who said *enough is enough* and create a sustainable peaceful energy and framework for your children's children to build on and maintain. That is what being a true hero for the planet is all about. Granted, it's not easy, but certainly something to strive for in every moment, in every day, year after year. Take one small step today towards creating peace in your life and then go to the next moment, in peace. This new practice *will* become a new habit, in time. Neuroplasticity and all that stuff. If you only read this paragraph and practice it, you will create a happy life for you and those around you. And you will in turn, become a leader the world most urgently needs right now. Thank you for considering this action for the greater good and for yourself. In the process of doing the research for this book, I looked for anything along similar topic lines that was already published. *The Politics of Love* by Marianne Williamson was published while I was writing this book. This new brand of politics is in the air and it really inspired me to see her book had just come out. I waited until I had finished writing my book to read Marianne's because there is nothing worse than accidental plagiarism. I want to mention *The Politics of Love* in my book as recommended reading, as it's really in tune with the principles I'm laying out here and gives an American perspective that I'm unable to give as someone who has lived under the Australian political system. I'm really grateful for Marianne's contribution to this peace and love style of politics, although our point of difference is that I'm including animals in my love and peace politics, in fact all living beings, whereas Marianne's book focuses primarily on human rights issues.

Get your communication skills sorted

Every great leader needs to learn to be an effective communicator. A comprehensive book on the subject is *Communicate : How to say what needs to be said, when it needs to be said, in the way it needs to be said,* by Clare Mann. If you have political ambitions or want to lead a social change group or movement, learning the art of great communication will advance your ambitions and outcomes tremendously.

Observing political candidates engage with voters is at times cringe-worthy and always eye-opening. It's crucial that political parties, even the micro ones, have social media etiquette training. As a mentor to first-time authors, a critical part of my advice to new authors is how to transition from member of the public to public figure. This is something that people new to politics really need to come to grips with. Arguing endlessly on Facebook about policy or issues with voters can be unprofessional and will be seen as such. Make your statement. Explain anything that appears to be unclear, and then let it rest. Communicate clearly and professionally and then leave it at that. You will gain a lot more respect that way.

Mem Davis is a writer and editor who is passionate about the topic of communicating clearly and with purpose:

"What if we could harness the power of language to create a kinder world?

What if our words could gather followers and create a community that seeks peace and compassion, rather than articulating our anger and rousing violence or dissension?

"Our words can drive people to make choices based on what is morally right rather than what they perceive to be the status quo. We can impart information with permission instead of aggression, and we can respond to questions and statements with facts and kindness instead of judgement and frustration. We can market to the mainstream and change the vocabulary of advertising.

"Imagine a world where marketing buzz words such as "cruelty-free", or "vegan" have real depth of meaning, and people's choices are informed by knowledge and a desire to do right by all living beings? We can make it so, by choosing to engage with positive and transformational language and by shaping our words with good intentions.

"Helping to create veganism as a mainstream option is a step towards a kinder world, and the power of words in doing so can't be underestimated. What we say and how we present ourselves to the world can be incredibly influential. I would love for each vegan voice to be heard clearly, and for words of compassion and kindness to spread wide and far."

About social media profiles

While we are on the subject: clean up your social media profiles if you are aiming for a leadership position of any kind, on any level. People are judging you, either consciously or subconsciously. For better or worse, this is true. Apart from professional communication, take note of what you are posting and what you are trying to achieve and portray about yourself.

Build social media profiles that communicate who you are and where you want to go. Be aspirational. Like the saying goes, you dress for the job you want to get, not for the one you are currently at.

Learn about personal branding. If you find this concept too commercial or icky (I did), then approach it from this angle: personal branding done well inspires confidence in others about you, it helps them feel comfortable. In this way, you are enhancing your cause, which could be the political party you are a member of or your animal rights event or your non-profit organisation. Whatever it is, it needs *you* to start acting professionally, if you aren't already, of course. Being strategic about personal branding helps you to be able to serve the community you aim to serve, as your consistent presence builds trust and thus opens up opportunities for you. Whenever I feel uncomfortable about branding and strategy I remember my purpose is to serve. It makes the process a lot easier to maintain.

From what you choose to wear, your personal grooming, your social media photos and commentary, it all matters. It all adds up to how people are perceiving you and ultimately whether they will buy from you or vote for you or attend your event. You are the front person for your stuff – so get that all in order, first and foremost.

Having said that, always be adaptable to the situation, the context, the culture and have situational awareness. Use common sense and intelligence to know when to do what. It's very important to be sensitive to a situation and context as it can make or break your campaign and/or aspirations.

An easy way to get started is to ask people what their perception of you is. Ask them to describe you in five words. Don't ask your mum or besties. Ask five random Facebook friends that you're not very close with in real life. Ask them for brutal honesty and work from there. If you think this stuff doesn't matter, you may not last long in public life.

As mentioned earlier, someone who does this all very well is Clare Mann, Psychologist, Speaker, Communications Trainer and Author of *Myths of Choice: Why People Won't Change and What You Can Do About It*. I asked Clare about what matters when it comes to communication and being an effective leader. This is what she said:

"As social creatures, each of us is eager to be significant, to be seen, to be important to others. This need is so great that some people sadly distort or hide who they are for fear of criticism, ridicule, or rejection. I have never seen this as a solution, for the cost of contorting ourselves into what is socially acceptable is great. We never reach our potential to offer our unique gifts to the world and, as a result, never feel seen.

"Historically, leaders were the only ones who held the compass and influenced others to go in a certain direction. To be an impactful leader in today's knowledge economy, it's not enough to know the facts and have a direction. Leadership is the ability to engage people at the emotional level, get them to buy into a worthy dream and appreciate that everything they do affects the process. Thus, high levels of ongoing self-reflection and responsibility are essential to lead and help others bring their unique gifts to the world.

"I believe true leadership comes from a generosity of heart and is actually not about being interested in leading at all, but rather assisting others to achieve a bigger vision. It requires a requisite set of skills of active listening, open-mindedness, curiosity, humility, encouraging people to contribute, and only giving energy to the outcome of the vision rather than fear that it may never materialise. For example, if we want a more just world, why spend time focusing on injustice at the expense of what a new era of justice will bring?

"Each of us has the ability to influence through our social interactions and to shine as the best example of ourselves, leading the way towards positive change in the world."

Presenting yourself as a professional person is not about fundamentally changing who you are, it's learning how to present yourself in the best possible way and communicating that effectively to your audience. If you're an ethical, really-good-for-the-world person, it's your duty to let everyone know that so they can follow you, vote for you, buy from you. If we are talking about elections, this is high stakes stuff. If a better presented person with no ethics and disastrous ideas and policy plans gets voted in because people had more faith in their ability based on the way they presented themselves and communicated, that's just a plain and simple tragedy. And people do vote in this way, sadly. But we can't complain, we just need to work smarter and turn this problem into an opportunity.

In the future, there will come a time when people are more intuitive, telepathic even (no, seriously), more connected to their hearts and souls, so maybe this personal branding stuff won't matter, but for now, it does matter, so we need to pay attention to it, for the sake of our causes.

Ethical leadership qualities

Believe it or not, politics can be done in an authentic, meaningful way. When imagining what future ethical political leaders would look like, the following qualities come to mind:

- Professional persona that inspires trust
- Relatable
- Approachable
- Personable
- Ethical in lifestyle and work
- Positive, determined outlook
- Problem solver
- Sees problems as opportunities
- Inspires confidence
- Inspires others to achieve their goals
- Has a solid, never give up mindset
- Polite and communicates well
- Strives for peace in all interactions. Doesn't look for conflict. Strives to find the common ground and works from that point.
- Defends the weak and vulnerable
- Works on subconscious influences to ensure actions and speech are in alignment with their higher self and life purpose.
- Committed to continuous personal growth
- Collaborative – even when in the highest positions of power and influence
- Lifts others up. Acts from their higher consciousness and not the lower feelings of fear and jealousy.
- Keeps the ego in check and maintains self awareness.
- Open to constructive feedback
- Compassionately governs; considers human and animal rights and planetary impact.
- Actively seeks to assist marginalised groups with the goal of equality for all
- Integrity, honesty, transparency, compassion, kindness towards all beings, gentleness and strength.

With parliaments across the world full of people with these qualities, we would certainly have the framework for a peaceful planet.

Where are the visionaries at?

What we need now more than ever before is people with vision. No vision is too grand or too out-of-the-box. We need people who are unafraid to share their big ideas, not water them down in the hope of winning votes. State your purpose. State your plan. Be bold and uncompromising. Don't think in terms of the next three to four years of your position. Leave a legacy and achieve real, solid improvements for your community, your country, the world.

We need leaders who are sensitive to how their decisions made today affect the world in 5, 10, 20, 100 years time. Who wants to be a leader that goes down in history as a narrow-minded, short term gain kind of leader? Apparently many. But it doesn't need to be that way forever. Stand tall and state your vision. Legacy over short term gain. We have the opportunity right now to create an ethical foundation for future generations. It's very easy in politics to lose sight of original intentions and values but it's not impossible to stick to them. It's time to get people excited and inspired about using their vote to create positive, sustainable, economically prosperous countries and planet.

It all begins with a vision. I'm not referring to rhetoric-filled speeches where slogans are repeated *ad nauseam* with no actual policy behind them. Real vision is authentic. It is detailed and is driven by unshakable passion. Within all of us we have a vision; an ideal of how we would like our life to be. If you've given up on that vision, or you've forgotten what your childhood dreams were, engage in the processing of recapturing that magic again.

Vision creates motivation. Motivation drives action. If we come from a place of deep vision, we can overcome any obstacles and arrive at our goal, in time.

Obviously, this is just a starting point for thinking about this topic. What qualities do you want to see in political leaders? What qualities do you want to further develop in yourself so you can become a more effective leader?

Ideology is not enough

It's absolutely essential to have strong ethics to be the leaders we need right now, and it's simply the compassionate, just way to be in any case. Along with ethics, we must also be strategic. If we are strong on ethics, but weak on strategy, we can only go so far. This means seeking to build alliances, not going around constantly looking for bridges to burn.

If someone doesn't have the ethical level you perceive to be good enough, but they are well on their way, give them a chance. Dialogue with them. You will be a much more effective activist, political candidate, or indeed an elected representative, if you are willing to sit down with people and work on relationship building. Please don't underestimate the power and importance of this skill set.

Mindset is everything

Tournament winning tennis players and other successful sportspeople are bagging those trophies because they are exceptional athletes with winning mindsets. Many of these winners invest as much in mindset coaching as they do in sports coaching. Why? Because what your mind is saying to you dictates the actions you take.

Some candidates will lose one election, give up and never stand as a candidate ever again. What is the difference between them and the person who keeps standing, election after election, until they win? Some might say ego, but often it is rather a purpose-filled determination to never give up which is coming from their mindset. They keep their mind as strong as possible.

In Jen Sincero's book, *You're A Badass At Making Money,* she talks a lot about visualisation as a tool for creating the reality and success you aspire to achieve. If that means imagining yourself sitting in parliament as a Senator, do this. Imagine all of the details. Your office, your staff, the legislation you are voting on, the powerful alliances you are forming. See it all coming to life. Visualisation is seriously powerful stuff and helps you become the person you wish to become and you'll be amazed how your subconscious mind starts to work for you to achieve the reality you have placed yourself in, in your mind.

Confidence

Back yourself. Believe in your potential and your incredible ability to overcome all obstacles in your path. When we do work that goes against the intrinsic grain of current society, we will face obstacles. Be prepared and work through it. We need you to keep going. Be among like-minded friends and colleagues who can buoy you up and encourage you when things get tough.

Ultimately, we are born alone and we die alone. You are all you've got. Become your own best friend. Champion yourself at all opportunities and remind yourself daily that you can do it. Whatever *it* is. Know that within you are incredible resources you can draw from to achieve your dreams.

Know when it's time to rest and allow that space to recover and rejuvenate.

Unshaken confidence in your ability, in your projects, in your vision, can mean the difference between finishing your project and giving up halfway. Remind yourself why it is important and what it means to you and those you are advocating for.

The power of presence

If a leader doesn't embody a strong leadership energy, voters will consciously or subconsciously pick up on it and won't vote for them because they won't feel confident in their ability to represent their concerns.

Policies are great, but you also need *presence*. When the policies are similar, the candidate with the strongest 'leadership aura' will win. They will attract the votes. You can either see this from a scientific or spiritual perspective; the end result is the same. Bonus points if you have charm, charisma, and a warm and relatable personality. It all helps.

The current problem is candidates with questionable ethics are winning political positions because they capture the trust of the people with the extraordinary confidence they have in themselves as leaders, whether this is justified or not.

You *must* believe in yourself and position every cell in your body, every thought that runs through your mind, towards seeing yourself as a great leader. It will create incredible shifts both inside and out. There are many tools you can use to create this result such as affirmations, visualisation, meditation, kinesiology, and leadership coaching with someone who has proven results in increasing confidence and presence in their clients.

It's quite hard to fake leadership presence. It's something to work on, alongside everything else you are doing to prepare to become a leader.

Being an inner or outer leader for peace

Those who lead ethically as elected representatives and leaders in business and charity do a great service to the world. Those who radiate peace through their sincere intention and prayers or through their dedicated spiritual practice, are the inner leaders for peace. The inner and outer leaders collectively form the team that brings hope, healing and justice to the world.

Become an action taker

Ideas are great. They are full of potential. But that's it. They don't go any further unless you take action on them. If I had a dollar for every time someone said they had a great idea for a book, or a business or non-profit organisation or something that sounded super great but went nowhere because that person didn't follow through, I'd be sitting comfortably on a big pile of 'ideas that went nowhere' cash. Follow. Through.

Write down, audio record, or video record your ideas. Ideas come to life once they are recorded. Once recorded, expand on that idea. Start brainstorming, no matter how wild and outrageous those subsequent ideas are, record them. Then start planning.

Planning assists in making ideas actionable and accountable. Those ideas need to go somewhere. Once you've decided your idea is viable, doable, awesome, and world-changing, implement it ASAP. Global urgent issues don't have time to wait for tomorrow. Implement today.

Focus

Value your time. Use it wisely. Instead of watching two hours of mindless television or online videos or aimlessly scrolling social media feeds, harness that time to implement one of your ideas. Life is a precious chance to help the world and initiate positive change. Value yourself as a co-creator in a world that is in the midst of an exciting positive shift. Join in and make a real difference. Focus your time and energy on the stuff that matters.

A note about writer's block

Mentoring first-time authors is something I really enjoy. I work with authors who have innovative ideas and are in the process of publishing their first book. One of the common obstacles they face is writer's block. It can significantly delay a project's completion and sometimes, if not dealt with effectively, can lead to a project being abandoned indefinitely.

Why does this happen? Many reasons. Sometimes it's fatigue. When our lives are so full already with work and family and other commitments, by the time we sit down for our allocated writing time, we are tired and lacking inspiration and the space for ideas to form into coherent sentences. The solution for this type of block is somehow getting more time to rest and be creative.

Being afraid to share your truth is another source of writer's block that writers may not be aware of immediately. It requires some honest self reflection and digging into why the words aren't flowing.

Other sources of writer's block are fear of success and fear of being seen and heard. These are common ones among women I have mentored and talked with on this topic. The mind may be battling with decades of gender expectations and role playing where they have seen themselves in a certain way (as a wife, a mother, a part-time worker to support their partner's main income). When the mindset shift occurs and they start to have grander visions of who they are and who they would like to become, the words start to flow as they allow themselves to be more than they've ever been before.

This is worthy of a mention here as there may be women who read this book and become inspired to take action and write their own books, start a blog, start a social justice campaign, develop a social media presence, start a non-profit organisation or business, enter politics or any of the many ways leadership can be expressed. They all require, to some degree, the ability to communicate with the written word. Removing the blocks or at least being aware that they exist and identifying what they might look like, can be very useful and time-saving when embarking on the leadership journey.

War and peace...and the Internet

In Jamie Bartlett's book, *The People vs Tech*, he talks about the effect social media has on democracy and voting decision making. Referencing Brexit, he makes the point that people will usually have a considered and mostly calm discussion with opposing voters around the dinner table, but during an internet discussion, it is more likely to become much more accusatory and aggressive. The ability to hide behind a keyboard is well known to create tension between people to a greater degree than it ever would in person, because facing someone in person is a whole different dynamic.

If we aim to create more peace on Earth, being aware of the instant-ness of social media interacting and how that tends to activate the emotional reptilian brain instead of the more logical, grounded part of ourselves, will go a long way in preventing online disagreements becoming all-out feuds. Keeping that in mind is essential to utilising the great benefits of connectivity social media provides without it becoming counter productive and ultimately creating more conflict.

Preparing to govern

People with big social media followings are doing great things at a grassroots level to inspire change. Changing our personal habits towards ethical ones is essential. In addition, the way the world is currently set up, the politicians have the power to change laws and thus decide the big biscuit stuff. That's why getting good people into decision-making positions matters. That's why you matter as a leader.

To prepare, learn as much as you can about economics and finance and other portfolios you will need to vote on when you're in parliament. Do this for the sake of the longevity, credibility, and ultimate success of the political party you represent and also so when people vote for you, you are doing your absolute best in that seat in parliament for the betterment of the nation. You are taking up a spot. Make it count.

Learning peace politics from the wise ones

I realise not everyone reading this book will be spiritually inclined, so I will just reference here one of the several enlightened Masters that has really made a big impact upon me, Lao Tzu. Spiritual teachers are great ones to learn from when preparing to be a leader. Their depth of understanding of the human predicament is vast.

The *Tao Te Ching* by Lao Tzu contains many excellent pieces of advice for leaders. This is one of my favourite quotes:

Those who wish to take the world and control it
I see that they cannot succeed
The world is a sacred instrument
One cannot control it
The one who controls it will fail
The one who grasps it will lose
Thus all things:
Either lead or follow
Either blow hot or cold
Either have strength or weakness
Either have ownership or take by force
Therefore the sage:
Eliminates extremes
Eliminates excess
Eliminates arrogance

Reprinted with permission
Derek Lim (taoism.net)

Dear introverts and highly sensitive souls...

As a fellow super introvert and sensitive, I know the struggle between wanting to contribute and wanting to be anonymous and blend into the crowd. I love staying home to enjoy unlimited tranquillity and privacy. However, taking small steps out of your comfort zone, in order to benefit the world, is a truly worthwhile pursuit. Introverts have a certain inner richness to offer the world, that is highly valuable and a much needed leadership quality.

In short, I'm inviting you to step up and step out into the world. Your contributions are valued and appreciated.

Here are some ways to kick start your stepping up and stepping out process:

1. Attend a small networking event with like-minded people. Commit to having one conversation with one person.
2. Go to a meetup where there is a discussion taking place and contribute one comment to the group discussion.
3. Give a short talk to a small number of people. A one minute talk to start.
4. If talking isn't an option, start writing a blog, book, or create a social media account.

And keep growing from there.

The future of politics is ethical vegans

I'll conclude this chapter with quotes from vegan members of parliament and vegan parliamentary candidates:

First up is a member of NSW (Australian) parliament, **The Hon. Emma Hurst MLC** from the **Animal Justice Party**:

"Since I can remember I have been deeply passionate about animal protection. A fierce campaigner during primary school and a proud vegan since my late teens, I have never once doubted that I wanted to dedicate my life to animal protection.

"Like many before me, my passion turned into my profession, and I have now been campaigning on behalf of animals for well over 15 years. But while every role has been another important step in the fight for a humane and ethical future, by far my most rewarding role has been the one I am in now – an MP for the Animal Justice Party.

"As a politician I have the immense privilege of being a voice for animals in parliament and ensuring they are top of mind in the decision making process. Here, I bring the message of the animals, the campaigners, and the community straight to the people who need to hear it most. The work I do every day makes real, legislative change that paves the way for animals to be protected by law now and into the future.

"Being a politician is in all respects very gratifying work, though that is not to say it is easy. My job, especially in my first term of Government, is to convince the hard right that animals are sentient and need protection. Thankfully, the tides are changing. With more of us in parliament, we are able to sway hearts, minds and legislation. And we are succeeding.

"We, as animal rights campaigners, activists and protectors know the future is ethical, humane and vegan. We are the leaders in a global movement for change. And it is clear to me that this change isn't just coming. It has arrived in politics not only here in Australia but across the globe, and it is undoubtedly because of all of us, that it is here to stay."

Clifton Roberts
Humane Party Presidential Candidate, US:

"As leaders, all of us need to fight, in whatever political capacity we can, to pass proposed changes to the Constitution. In order to win at passing national legislation, we must win by strategically embedding ethical champions throughout the chambers of Congress.

"Join the political movement(s) calling for ending inhumane, scientifically indefensible, and economically unsound exploitation of other species by humans, which includes the elimination of domestic trade and import/export of sentient beings; the elimination of torture, mutilation, and slaughter of such beings; the elimination of domestic and foreign trade in products resulting from or obtained by way of such exploitation; the elimination of services that include or are provided by way of such exploitation, including experiments performed on live animals and entertainment events that include live animals; abolishing the property status of, and emancipating, other animals by either explicitly recognizing all other animals as fully protected individuals under the 13th Amendment prohibition of slavery, or ratifying a new Constitutional amendment emancipating all other animals through proposed Constitutional amendments that propose to grant legal standing and personhood to all other animals, such that an animal's liberty can be procured by way of a habeas corpus proceeding and his or her rights can be enforced through a duly authorized legal guardian.

"What to do?

"Run for local, state, or federal office. You have nothing to lose but to lose. If you lose, try until you win—you have everything to gain by being the political voice of animals and being immortalized on the right side of history books. Furthermore, learn about the elected officials who represent you. What are the personal and business interests of your representatives? Will this person represent your interest to the extent that animal rights, the environment, and free speech is involved?"

Professor Andrew Knight MANZCVS, DipECAWBM (AWSEL), DipACAW, PhD, FRCVS, SFHEA
Animal Welfare Party (UK) 2019 General Election Candidate:

"From 2007 – 2012 I was a Spokesperson for the Animal Welfare Party (then Animals Count); a British political party for people and animals. Based on the highly successful Dutch Party for the Animals, the party aims to raise the status of animal issues within UK politics and legislation, and has inspired and assisted the establishment of political parties for animals in other countries. I've been an electoral candidate for the Party in three general elections, and one EU parliamentary election. In 2017 I stood against the Prime Minister Theresa May, in her home constituency. We received more votes than any of the other minor parties, emphasizing the importance of animal welfare, and helping to ensure her party thereafter dropped its plans to reintroduce fox-hunting.

"In the 2019 general election I enjoyed huge success in hustings events, by calling for simple decency in the way we treat other animals, because it is the right thing to do. That really resonated with people, and everyone was thereafter thinking about animal welfare. That's the kind of impact we want to make. It's a great opportunity for building invaluable experience as well, e.g. in public speaking. I advise animal advocates everywhere to consider the benefits of becoming involved in politics – although it is important to also consider the time and money required, and whether you can have greater impact elsewhere. Our impact in 2019 made it worthwhile, but that will not always be the case. It's also important not to split the progressive vote, in any marginal seat. We chose ours carefully, to avoid any such risk."

Maneka Gandhi
Member of Lok Sabha, Lower House of Parliament, India:

"The struggle has to be a political one. You have no impact if you go the consumer route. The government doesn't care which lipstick you buy. It will be a thousand years before you, as consumers, make any dent in the lipstick market which has not reduced the number of lipsticks that use beeswax and gelatin but expanded it to meet your lipstick needs. But if you were to make a group that votes determinedly for people who will stop meat export and shut down slaughterhouses and legislates on what lipsticks can be in the market, then your veganism would have some meaning.

"While becoming vegan is important in the step towards saving the planet, the minute you go looking for 'cruelty free underwear', you have lost the battle. You don't need more goods, vegan or otherwise, that deplete resources, pollute ecosystems, fill landfills, and kill free-living nonhumans— you need less of everything.

"Veganism is about dismantling a system that depends on the enslavement and abuse of nonhuman lives. If you are to be vegan then be so in every capacity; reducing or eliminating your travel, your reproduction, consumption, waste. You need to be politically informed and active and engaging others, being willing to take a stand and speak out. And you need to rescue animals.

"To commit to veganism is good, but it is just the starting point to a more nonviolent and just world. We need to educate, disrupt, resist, confront, and change institutions that shape policies and culture and make animal abuse possible in the first place. It's a tall order that requires discipline and courage, not vegan ice-cream.

"Decide what your issues are and what difference you can reasonably make with the time and energy you have available. What are your skills? Who else can you get involved? What effect do you want to have?"

Chapter Six

Step Into the World of Peace on Earth:
a story of what could be

by Flavia Ursino Coleman

Story time.

The following fictional story describes two scenarios and represents the fact that the choices we make create the world we live in. Do we choose ethical, inspired leadership, or greedy, self-entitled leadership?

All around the world, governments were scrambling to protect the people. An unprecedented cascading series of events had plunged the world into a mood of sombre darkness and despair. Time had appeared to quicken, as if spinning in onto itself at a dizzying pace, while populations contributed their compulsory twelve hour day working shifts. Month after month seemed to fly off the calendar; the commencement of each new year tinged with some vague hope of a better to come.

A scorching winter had morphed into a frost bitten spring, followed by a mild and almost bearable autumn orbiting back into a heat stricken winter. Earthquakes, raging fires, dust storms, volcanic eruptions and angry seas were now almost daily occurrences with several events recorded most days. Globally the ground as a whole had become parched and hostile to crop production. What little survived was treated with careful handling and packaging. Food security had become a preoccupation for the majority. Soon food rations would be introduced in order to ensure better welfare standards and equal distribution. The initial quota of food and other resources were given over to the elite and those said to have been assigned the right to rule. Secret stores of food, water and other supplies were hoarded in secret locations. Those in positions of rulership saw no necessity in disclosing what had been stored, the amount nor the whereabouts. In order to meet water demands, animals had been bred as drought resistant with many more as interspecies hybrids. They had been bred and raised as warehouses for failing organs to meet consumer demands for the wealthy in need of such transplants as kidneys and livers.

Child protection services wasted no time in removing children at risk of malnourishment and improper health care from their homes and their parents were charged for crimes of abuse and neglect. In a number of countries dwindling water supplies had led to a surge in criminal behaviour. Youth gangs classed as terrorists had begun breaking into people's homes in order to steal what little water they could siphon from rain water tanks. Governments, had begun taking necessary measures to forcibly remove water tanks from properties and issuing hefty fines with jail sentences for repeat offenders and for those who repeatedly defied the law by choosing to store rain water.

With the escalation of violence, it was only a matter of time before lives would be lost. Advanced technology had made it relatively easy to catch terrorists in the act. Street security cameras attached to communication equipment had almost perfected facial and voice recognition which would alert the authorities within minutes of any unlawful conduct. Frivolous desires for personal freedom and personal rights had given way to the need for safety and security for all global citizens, for the greater good.

Getting through such severe times called for severe and responsible measures which had been encouraged as a global collective effort to stamp out anti-social behaviour. All communications were monitored and recorded. Consequently, law abiding citizens were rewarded by the knowledge that a number of heinous crimes such as rape and kidnap had declined with futuristic crime figures predicted to show an all time low, trending towards an optimistic outlook of eventually stamping out such horrific events throughout the world.

Suddenly the room swayed violently! Gasping for air, Maggie sat bolt upright. Her heart racing incredibly fast as if it had somewhere else to go. Conscious of each breath she worked to reorientate herself in her surroundings. It was that recurring nightmare. "Damn!", she uttered. Each dream seemed to present with an increased sense of urgency. She attempted to relax every muscle in her body, muscle by muscle as she lowered herself back into a restful position. Conscious of her unborn baby kicking she continued to draw in breath and to breathe out deeply.

Juxtaposed this dystopian nightmare, was a utopian dream of joy, and peace, where humans participated in a harmonious world of abundance, for all beings, where plant food nourished the body and what few ailments that may have presented were healed by naturally growing herbs.

The elements were in harmony with regular and predictable seasons that produced food in great quality and quantity. Abundance too was in large measure created by working in harmony with water, fire, earth and air. Being in sync with each element allowed for the rightful times of planting, growth and harvest. While each grew their own, all was shared. Scarcity was unknown. They also utilised the elements in order to cool, heat, wash, and to power transportation and machinery.

Led by intuitive forces, women held the greater authority throughout the world. They did not seek to rule as such, but rather to organise by way of connection, collaboration, and cooperation. These wise women led the world as vegan leaders of world peace. Gentle voices won greater persuasion than any form of austere rulership could have ever hoped to achieve.

The fruitful bearings of Mother Earth's womb were worshipped and each life considered sacred. All animals were revered and free to roam. They expressed themselves through their individual uniqueness. Interspecies communication was perceived through the eyes and each connected through soul love and understanding. Humans had become wise and gentle and all life thrived in an enriched environment. Unafraid, animals who found themselves in peril would signal for human assistance. The animal kingdom rewarded their human cousins many times over as they too could sense any human in need of comfort.

Feminine wisdoms of birth, nurture, growth, death, and regeneration were held as the highest of all governing principles. Without the delicate balance of love and nurture all of Mother Earth's children would over time perish. Women understood this both deeply and instinctively and as such organised themselves around earth's needs. Crime was unknown as cooperation held higher esteem over competition.

Both humans and non humans moved about from zone to zone in a leisurely manner. Communication was light hearted and all were heard. Words were used richly and wisely and had an almost melodic composition about them.

It was rumoured that the then people often viewed tea and sympathy as time consuming and menacing. The people were said to have consumed chemical compounds due to stress and loneliness. Babies and children were said to have been raised away from the family and the elderly discarded as they awaited their deaths.

Yet here, the broader community loved, cherished and embraced intergenerational living. The young kept them laughing and vibrant and the elderly were honoured amongst the community for their wisdom passed down through their story telling.

Female leaders knew that the cornerstone of a happy and well balanced world was in taking great care with those most vulnerable. Children were raised to trust those older than themselves and to know the world as a safe place. Children expressed themselves creatively and their talents were nurtured. This would in time assist them in giving back to the world in which they were born and that had given them so much. They understood their value as human beings and grew to stand within their power. Truth was what they were told and truth was what they had known and each spoke their truth with great eloquence. They meditated and had vision for their journey knowing always that divine energy would guide them and was always available to manifest the greater good for themselves and others. Their higher potential would mark out their road through life and each had a vision for their future.

Non-selective compassion was taught in all schools and upheld as the highest of core values. Respect for all life regardless of form and outer appearance remained a constant, nurtured by the broader community. Through female leadership the world remained an uncomplicated place. The primary needs of humans were fulfilled. Each human had access to food, water, warmth, rest, shelter, safety, security, love, community and in return gave back of themselves into the cycle of abundance.

They did not bemoan illness as the leaders encouraged the basic principles of health; clean water, movement, meditation, alkalinity and nutrition. They had clean air to breathe, sunshine, exercise when they had energy and rest when they did not, temperance, an unrefined vegan diet, clean water, and trust in a divine power. They fasted when ill and listened to their bodies at all times. These female leaders had health care plans not sickness care plans. All health was considered natural health and rumours of how humanity once believed in unnatural health were responded to with bellowing laughter that could be heard throughout the community. They had great faith in the human body and understood that humans are self-developing, self-defending and self-repairing, provided that all the elements for health were present.

Each had knowledge that health and abundance was indeed their birthright that should not be interfered with. Each lived close to the greater spirit and each knew how to call upon the greater power rather than compete and take from others. Subsequently humans aged more slowly and gracefully. They were energy givers, not energy stealers. They knew nothing of stress and they empowered each other. After all, the giving was rich and the gains even richer.

In this civilisation there was no shame of the human body nor shame of the tender heart as neither were given over to exploitation. Humans weren't carved up into body parts such as breasts and bottoms plastered on billboards in order to sell everything from hotdogs to hot cars. Humans were honoured in their entirety; mind, body and soul. Relationships if falling beneath the natural state of soul deep connection were repaired not replaced.

People danced in the rain and the warmth of sun beams danced on their glowing skin. Colours were vibrant and alive unhampered by smoke and pollution. Unity kept every individual safe and freedom of unique self expression was encouraged and nurtured. Differences of opinions quickly gave way to humour, growth and understanding. The people laughed often and loudly. Little was taken seriously and patience was in endless supply. Love was an ever present force that guided one's path and each path held the story of the one who walked it and it was considered sacred.

People of the world framed their lives within the three codes for living which replaced the laws of justice. Code 1: Strive to be happy. Code 2: Strive to take good care of ourselves and our families. Code 3: Give something back.

Naturally happy, healthy people always enjoyed giving back in a world where individual talents were nurtured. Contribution to the collective flowed without effort and was given with joyful hearts. Everyone had that special something to contribute be it that of helping nurture an infant, the fine mind of a mathematician, or the glorious voice that filled the air with delight. God-given talents were the social currencies that held the community together. It had been said that the previous society had traded on greed and that many had suffered dreadfully through exhaustion and poverty. If in fact this society had once existed, how could they have not seen that both poverty consciousness and elitism were twins of the same fictitious human creation? Both held beliefs of lack rather than the acknowledgement of the birthright of abundance. It was hard to imagine that the people were not governed by their birthrights of health and happiness too. Did they not understand the principles of unity and cooperation? Perhaps this is why that society had collapsed and disappeared. Did they not take in the secret of life which had been so clearly inscribed on each tomb? "In loving memory." The meaning of life could not have been more clearly written. But then again those tomb stones may too have been nothing more than rumours.

Time had slowed down it seemed as Maggie awaited her child's birth, until she was eventually presented with a beautiful baby girl. It had been a longish delivery and after breastfeeding, both mother and child rested peacefully side by side. Lovingly Maggie watched her baby's sweet blue eyes flutter into a sleep. Mesmerised she looked into them deeply when suddenly it came to her. Those reoccurring dreams! They were dreams of two paths. Each path held life choice and the world she would help create for her daughter. Which path would Maggie take?

Final Words

This book has been the most interesting publishing project I have ever undertaken. When I started researching and writing, it all came through very quickly and effortlessly, almost like an invisible force of inspiration was encouraging me and guiding my every word and sentence. But that's enough about me and the process. This book serves as a very basic introduction to golden age politics ideas. I didn't even touch on the media's effect on the outcome of elections, which is probably a whole other book in itself.

I've included a list of references in the back here, in case you want to read in more detail, some of the topics or sources discussed. As stated in the introduction, my hope was that this book has bolstered your hope, re-inspired the weary and ignited passion in the previously apathetic.

Whatever your case, I hope you've come away, at the very least, with the notion that politics can be a dynamic, energy filled and interesting process to engage in, and that the possibilities are infinite and dare I say, wondrous and exciting. We are constantly co-creating our existence on Earth every time we vote; with our purchasing power and with our ballot papers. May we decide ethically, responsibly, and compassionately at every step.

Thank you for joining me on this journey. If you made it to the end of the book, and got something out of it, I'd much appreciate it if you could spread the word via a review online or by sharing it on your social media pages. I can add your review to my website, to future editions of this book and on my social media pages. Together we are stronger! Thank you.

I wish all ethical political candidates, elected representatives, community leaders and all others with ethical leadership aspirations however big or small, the very best in all you do. Thank you for making this world a better place for all beings. May you be blessed and protected always.

Thank you

Kathy Divine

For peaceful and inspiring connecting and collaborating:

@itskathydivine

facebook.com/itskathydivine

@kathydivine
@australianvegans

/kathydivine

kathy@kathydivine.com

www.kathydivine.com

Acknowledgements

To all great leaders throughout history who fearlessly stepped outside the norm of their era and exhibited pioneering and compassionate, ethical leadership, thank you all. You inspire me everyday with your courage, determination and ethics. Leaders come in many forms, including Kings, Queens, Prime Ministers, Presidents, community leaders, parents and school teachers. Others spiritually lead humankind into higher consciousness. They are all my heroes.

I'm merely the little instrument who put this book together. I cannot emphasise this enough. I've been aided by many people, both past and present. Past through the work they have left behind, and present with physical assistance, written contributions, reviews, research, and physical work others have done in the background. Most significantly, the writing of this book was often effortless on my part due to guidance from many directions. There are no words to express this aspect. Any praise for this book can be offered to the Universal Love which surrounded me during the time of writing and preparation. Whether you call that force God, or Allah, or Buddha or simply Love Eternal, I am grateful for that loyal companion and guide and all good reviews should go in that direction. Any complaints or criticisms can be passed onto 'me' as the imperfect, often times, clumsy instrument.

This book was to a large extent inspired by my spiritual Master, Supreme Master Ching Hai and Her slogan *Be Vegan Make Peace*. I will be forever grateful for Her wise, guiding influence and Her mighty example of ethical leadership across multiple domains including, but not limited to, spiritual, creative, business, humanitarian and animal rights and welfare.

Thank you to the dedicated nun at Plum Village who assisted me in including Thich Nhat Hanh's wise words in the book.

Additional and significant influences have been varied and surprising. In the course of the research and reflection process for this book, I came across outstanding individuals who have deeply shaped my perspectives and the finished product you have in your hands right now. In no particular order, former US President Abraham Lincoln, St. Joan of Arc, Madame Blavatsky, Lao Tzu, St Francis of Assisi, Joseph Smith, Mohammed, Mother Mary and Jesus Christ. They are all, for different reasons, leaders I am grateful to for their work and dedication to creating a world of higher consciousness, peace and happiness for all beings.

My mum, Jenny Doyle, for assisting in the research and granting me access to her extensive library. When everyone else was giving up their books and going digital, thank you for standing your ground and keeping all the books you somehow knew I would need one day.

Thanks to my dad, Denis Doyle, for exposing me to politics at a young age and to the politicians I met during childhood who gave me my first impressions of what it's like behind the scenes of the political process. There's no way I could have written a book on this topic without growing up in a political family. That kind of first-hand education has played an invaluable part in shaping my thoughts and ultimately, the motivation to create this book. It took me four decades to figure out how I feel about politics and what I want to contribute, but it all began from those first impressions as a kid, so my gratitude to everyone I met from that age onwards who helped steer me in my current direction. They don't necessarily align with my viewpoint now at all, but I am still grateful for their influence. Everyone is a teacher, in one way or another.

In creating this book, I'm grateful for the team I've been lucky enough to work with. My designer Carolina Garzón has been instrumental with her incredible talent and encouragement. Bianca Harman, for typing some of my initial, scribbled notes. Penny Rowe for her administration assistance, deep discussions and insightful, talented editing that was invaluable in shaping numerous parts of the book. Her writing and input on the topics of gun control and education were particularly appreciated and valued. Penny's awareness of Plum Village assisted me in reaching out to Thich Nhat Hanh for a quote from him. Thank you very much to Mem Davis for her editing and proofreading work. Lynn Bain, thank you for your inspiration, encouragement and input. Thank you to Dr Natalie Kladnitski for your strategy advice and support.

To everyone who reviewed the book, thank you all. To the contributors for believing in me and unconditionally adding your wise words to the book, thank you. Special mention to Flavia Ursino Coleman for her story and for believing in the vision of this book.

Thank you to Marcos Ortega Ramirez, Founder and Vice-President of V Market Korea (http://vegbox.kr) for your overall support for the project, and other friends, too many to name.

For anyone who actually read this page and didn't skip over it, thank you for taking this moment to read this acknowledgement of these amazing souls.

Introducing the Inspiration for my Work

For the past 23 years I've practiced the inner light and sound meditation under the guidance of Supreme Master Ching Hai. It's been the one constant in my life that has lovingly steered me through all the ups and downs of this human existence. My connection to the Universal Love and Peace that dwells within all of us, has grown stronger as every day passes thanks to this meditation practice. It's an ancient, sacred spiritual practice taught by all great Masters of all times.

Apart from being a spiritual Master, Supreme Master Ching Hai is a renowned artist, best-selling author, poet, film producer, the founder of Supreme Master Television and international chain of vegan restaurants, Loving Hut. She has won several awards across creative, leadership and world peace categories including the Gusi Peace Prize (2006), the World Spiritual Leadership Award (1994) and the World Citizen Humanitarian Award (1994).

The inspiration for my work has all manifested as a result of this daily meditation practice. All of the courage and determination has come from having this inner connection with God. None of the books or the magazines or anything else I've done or will ever do, would have happened or will happen without the practice of this most powerful meditation. I owe it all to the Master's power and the Grace of God who blesses my life daily. For me, I've learnt that leadership is firstly an inside job that then reflects upon the outer actions: cultivate myself first so I may be of service to others afterwards. This is what Confucius taught and it still holds true today.

For more information, please visit:

www.godsdirectcontact.org

About Noteworthy News on Supreme Master Television

Noteworthy News is broadcast on Supreme Master Television and provides a daily dose of positive and inspiring news from around the globe. The latest environmental initiatives, pioneering vegan projects and all manner of other things that are good for humanity, animals and the planet are broadcast on this international news program. This news is deeply researched to cover countries that you rarely, if ever, hear about on mainstream media outlets. There is positive stuff happening absolutely everywhere on this beautiful planet. This is world peace broadcasting at its finest. Noteworthy News on Supreme Master Television serves to bring the world together in greater understanding of each other and what we all have in common: a sincere desire to be happy, healthy and live meaningful lives.

You can catch Noteworthy News on the Supreme Master Television network every hour or so, 24/7. Watching this news everyday is truly refreshing because of the multicultural, positive approach to news broadcasting. After a week of daily watching, you will certainly feel the positive shift within yourself.

To watch Noteworthy News and the other uplifting programs on Supreme Master Television, please visit: www.suprememastertv.com

Index of Contributors

(Listed alphabetically by surname)

Connect with the Contributors

(Listed alphabetically by surname)

Flavia Ursino Coleman

Flavia Ursino Coleman is a spiritual advisor, teacher and lecturer of forty years. Holding a vision for a world beyond suffering to a world of non-selective compassion where all life is cherished and held as sacred. Flavia has chosen to utilise her 'word privilege' in order to raise awareness of those who cannot speak for themselves through her teachings, poetry and novel writing. Flavia has co-authored a novel *Monkey Business: A Story of Soulmates and Primates* with her husband, retired medical doctor Kevin Coleman.

www.monkeybusinessthebook.com

Mem Davis

Mem Davis is a writer and editor who speaks the language of the vegan community. She believes in supporting independent and ethical businesses with the intention of driving the economy based on moral choice over mere convenience.

www.memdavis.com

Billie Dean

Billie is a writer, innate interspecies telepath, globally respected animal shaman and social visionary. She founded the Deep Peace Trust, a social change organisation, supporting A Place of Peace, Australia's largest farm animal and wild horse sanctuary, created and run by Billie, her husband Andrew, and daughter Tamsin. The Trust is also home to the Billie Dean School of Wyld Shamanism which teaches ancient wisdom and new thought for deeper connections to the animals, nature and the unseen. Billie and Andrew also founded the vegan-friendly story studio Wild Pure Heart.
www.deeppeacetrust.com, www.wildpureheart.com, www.billiedean.com

Katrina Fox

Katrina Fox is an award-winning journalist, PR consultant, founder of
VeganBusinessMedia.com, host of Vegan Business Talk podcast and author
of *Vegan Ventures: Start and Grow an Ethical Business,* the first global book
providing success strategies for aspiring and existing vegan business owners.
She has written extensively for niche and mainstream media for 18 years on
animal advocacy and ethical business and was a regular Forbes contributor
specialising in writing about vegan and plant-based businesses. A vegan of
22 years, Katrina provides resources and training to vegan entrepreneurs,
including teaching them how to do their own PR and get free media coverage
through her signature online course and group coaching program Vegans in
the Limelight. She loves glitter, bling and disco.

www.katrinafox.com and www.veganbusinessmedia.com

Maneka Gandhi

Maneka Gandhi is an Indian politician and animal rights activist. She has
been a minister in four governments and has authored a number of books
concerning the areas of etymology, law and animal welfare. Maneka Gandhi
has been the recipient of numerous awards relating to the environment,
animal welfare and vegetarianism. Maneka Gandhi runs an NGO, People for
Animals.

People for Animals also known as PFA is India's largest animal welfare
organization with a nationwide network of 26 hospitals, 165 units and 2.5
Lakh members. They work to rescue and rehabilitate sick and needy animals.
In addition, they set up and run shelters, ambulance services, sterilization
programs, treatment camps and disaster rescue missions for animals. They
also conduct education programs in schools, fight cases in court and lobby
on animal issues in parliament.

www.peopleforanimalsindia.org

Aunty Ro Mudyin Godwin

Aunty Ro Mudyin Godwin is a proud Palawa Woman and Founder of Wugongga Kangaroo Group, NSW. An Initiated Teacher of Traditional Knowledge of Kangaroo and Country, she has been involved in exposing the reality of the repugnant Kangaroo Killing Industry for over forty years.

The Hon. Emma Hurst, MLC

The Hon. Emma Hurst is a Member of the Legislative Council in the Parliament of New South Wales, Australia, representing the Animal Justice Party. She has been a passionate campaigner for animal rights since childhood, and has previously worked as Campaign Director for Animal Liberation and Media Officer at PETA.

During her career, Emma has run a number of successful campaigns, putting an end to cruel wild goat racing, ensuring multiple companies cease their sales of rabbit meat, and rescuing hundreds of animals from medical research. As an MP, she has continued to fight for animals by securing parliamentary inquiries into battery cage hens, the use of animals in entertainment, and ag-gag laws in NSW.

Cassy Judy

Cassy Judy is a criminal lawyer and musician. She believes in the law as a tool to enhance social justice. She has worked for Legal Aid NSW, the Aboriginal Legal Service and Victims Services.

As a musician, her songs are lyrically brilliant and catchy, replete with witticisms from her life as a transgender woman, criminal lawyer and ocean adventurer! Cassy regularly performs at Trans Glamore, Chicks with Picks, Vegan Open Mic and Parliament on King. She recently performed her song, "Last Night" at the Broken Heel festival to a delighted audience. A proud vegan, Cassy spoke at the 2018 Plant Powered Women Leadership Conference on Transgender Awareness. She continues to work to increase the visibility of Trans and Gender Diverse people.

web: www.cassyjudy.com
Insta: @cassyjudymusic

FB: www.facebook.com/cassyjudymusic

Betska K-Burr

Betska is Co-President at Coaching and Leadership International Inc. She is the developer of 80+ award-winning coaching and leadership methodologies called The Science of Mind-Kinetics®. Betska is an International Trainer, Consultant, Speaker, Coach and confidante to individuals in 50+ countries: CXO's, Senior Government officials, Middle Managers, Ambassadors, Royalty, TV News Anchors, Star Athletes, troubled teens, street people, the addicted and abused, and brain injured, to name a few. She is a Canadian best-selling author of many books and multiple business award winner including 2019 "Top 100 Management Consultants in the World" by CEO Today Magazine. Betska is an avid gardener, loves to hike and create healthy vegan food for her family, and has an undeniable weakness for dark chocolate! To register for the "Women Rise & Lead" on-line program, https://cli-global.com/lead-basecamp-registration

www.CoachingAndLeadership.com

Professor Andrew Knight

Andrew Knight is a ridiculously busy bloke. He is Professor of Animal Welfare and Ethics, and Founding Director of the Centre for Animal Welfare, at the University of Winchester; a EBVS European and RCVS Veterinary Specialist in Animal Welfare Science, Ethics and Law; an American and New Zealand Veterinary Specialist in Animal Welfare; a Fellow of the Royal College of Veterinary Surgeons, and a Senior Fellow of the UK Higher Education Academy.

Andrew has over 65 academic publications and a series of YouTube videos on animal issues. These include an extensive series examining the contributions to human healthcare of animal experiments, which formed the basis for his 2010 PhD and his 2011 book *The Costs and Benefits of Animal Experiments*. Andrew's other publications have examined the contributions of the livestock sector to climate change, vegetarian companion animal diets, the animal welfare standards of veterinarians, and the latest evidence about animal cognitive and related abilities, and the resultant moral implications. His informational websites include www.AnimalExperiments.info, www. HumaneLearning.info and www.VegePets.info.

Jenny McCracken

Jenny McCracken, is an environmental activist and visual artist, and regards herself as an 'artivist'. Her father was a horticulturist, committed to growing crops for market in the least intrusive manner possible. Jenny has involved herself in climate activism for 12 years, in numerous projects including National Climate Action Summits, and the Darebin Climate Action Network, always as the lonely voice of veganism in the pioneering stages, where people were yet to make the connection between food choice and environmental impact. As a commercial and public artist, Jenny is always looking for opportunities to weave environmental messages into her work wherever possible.

E: jam2arts@mac.com
W: jennymccrackenartist.com
Insta: @jennymccrackenartist

Clare Mann

Clare Mann is an Australian-based psychologist, communications trainer and leadership consultant with extensive international experience in individual, group and organisational development. She has been awarded fellowships to both the Australian Human Resources Institute and the British Psychological Society for her contribution to those professions. Beyond her work which clearly sits inside an ethical leadership model, Clare is an ethical vegan and a staunch defender of animal rights. She has studied the psychology of ethical veganism for over a decade and has contributed much to understanding its ethical imperative through her definitive work *Vystopia: The Anguish of Being Vegan in a Non-Vegan World* (2018). https://claremann.com

Palak Mehta

Palak Mehta started India's leading vegan publication and solution space

Vegan First in 2016. Vegan First is an active enabler of the plant-based ecosystem in India by helping people choose a more conscious lifestyle through vegan alternatives and providing support. Drawing inspiration from nature, animals and children, Palak built her foundation on reimagining ways to live in Urban India. Palak has worked as an artist, teacher and permaculturalist, taking part in multiple group exhibitions and a solo exhibition. She represents the Indian chapter of the World Vegan Organisation, a global body of vegan-friendly thought leaders and industry experts.

www.veganfirst.com

Victoria Moran

Listed among *VegNews* magazine's "Top 10 Living Vegetarian Authors," voted Peta's "Sexiest Vegan Over 50" in 2016, and featured twice on *Oprah*, Victoria Moran has written thirteen books, including the iconic *Main Street Vegan* and the international bestseller, *Creating a Charmed Life.* She hosts the award-winning Main Street Vegan podcast; is producer of the 2019 documentary, *A Prayer for Compassion,* about spirituality and food choices; and she is director of Main Street Vegan Academy, the exciting, in-person certification program training Vegan Lifestyle Coaches and Educators in a magical week in New York City.

www.mainstreetvegan.net

Tracie O'Keefe

Dr Tracie O'Keefe DCH, BHSc, ND, is a clinical hypnotherapist, psychotherapist and counsellor with over 25 years' experience in full-time clinical practice. She is also a trained naturopath with a degree in complementary medicine. Before coming to Australia in 2001 she worked for many years at the London Medical Centre as a clinical hypnotherapist, psychotherapist and counsellor and is now the director of the Australian Health and Education Centre, Sydney. She has seen over 20,000 patients in her clinics, helping them to achieve happy, healthy lives, is the author of nine books, hundreds of articles and creator of a range of downloadable self-help programs.

www.tracieokeefe.com – hypnotherapy, psychotherapy clinic
www.healtheducationcentre.com – naturopathy, nutrition clinic
www.doctorok.com – downloadable self-help programs and hypnotherapist masterclasses

Lorraine Palmer

Lorraine Palmer is a healthy lifestyle creator and plant based food chef, mentor and author of the book *Raw Food In A Flash*. She has been featured in *Chat*, *Daily Mail* and graced the front cover of *Wolverhampton (lifestyle) Magazine* and appeared on countless live stream shows talking about the wonders of eating plant based foods. Eating this way relieved her own menopausal symptoms and fuelled her passion to disseminate this information to all. She currently offers a transformational program aimed at women who want to change the way they eat and adopt a healthier, sustainable diet. https://www.lorrainepalmer.com/raw-food-flash/

Dr Tamasin Ramsay

Dr Tamasin Ramsay had a career as a Melbourne paramedic before earning her doctorate in medical anthropology. She then worked at the United Nations in New York representing civil society and raising awareness of the climate emergency, caused in large part by systems, structures and industries that routinely exploit non-human animals. Dr Ramsay now proudly works with Animal Justice Party Member of Parliament Mr Andy Meddick, MLC (Western Victoria) as his Research and Policy Advisor. From participating in frontline actions and fostering rescued animals, to bringing the words of kindness and rationality into the chambers of parliament, she remains an activist dedicated to representing the interests of animals on their terms and will not stop until they are free.

Clifton Roberts

In his current role as Global Director of Public Policy for the world's largest producer of Semiconductors, Clifton advocates for public policy that is technology-neutral, while protecting consumer rights.

In 2016, Clifton became the Humane Party's first candidate for President of the United States of America. In 2018, Roberts became the party's first ever candidate for United States Senate. Clifton sits on the Board of Directors for In Defense of Animals and Lakewood College in Ohio.

Information on Clifton's vision for a prosperous, sustainable, and cruelty-free economy is being made available through the official website for his Political campaigns – www.cliftonroberts.org.

Penny Rowe

Penny Rowe is a writer, editor and cartoonist with a passion for social justice, animal rights, nutrition and natural history. A vegan since 2009, she currently lives in Sydney with her daughter.
Contact Penny via penelopeerowe@gmail.com

Zoe Simmons

Zoe Simmons is a journalist and copywriter with a passion for making a difference. She believes writing can change the world, or at least someone's world: and she wants to be a part of that. Having published her first article at the tender age of 16, Zoe has now been published hundreds of times around the globe—and she's never looked back. www.zoesimmons.com.au

Claire Smith

Claire Smith is a financial professional with 35 years experience in financial markets, initially as an investment banker and latterly as an investment consultant, specializing in complex trading strategies. In 2017, she started her own investment firms, under the banner Beyond Investing, with the intention of launching both public and private markets investment programs. In the public markets space, the flagship is the US Vegan Climate ETF (ticker: VEGN) launched in September 2019, and in the private markets she has been constructing programs that invest in companies that are producing plant-based, cruelty-free and animal-replacing products that accelerate our transition to a compassionate world, free of animal exploitation, since 2017. In addition, she is chair of Beyond Animal, an online tech community and funding platform designed to promote the growth of the vegan economy.

Dr Aryan Tavakkoli MRCP FRACP CFMP

Dr Tavakkoli is a consultant physician and medical director of Quantum Clinic in East Sussex, UK, a progressive medical clinic offering an integrative and functional medicine approach to people with cancer.
Dr Tavakkoli provides a multi-faceted approach to cancer, including oncothermia, mistletoe therapy, oxygenation therapy, intravenous vitamin therapy, metabolic pathway blockers, phytonutrient supplements, whole food plant-based nutrition, gut health, micronutrient optimisation, and mind-body therapy.

Her aim is to approach the problem at the root level and therefore enable her patients to achieve long term wellness and a better quality of life than would be achieved by using an allopathic medical approach alone.

https://quantumclinic.co.uk/

Further Reading and Bibliography

Business and Employment

Fox, Katrina. *Vegan Ventures: Start and Grow An Ethical Business.* O'Keefe and Fox Industries, Pty Ltd, 2015

https://www.businessinsider.com.au/plant-based-meat-market-australia-cut-back-meat-free-diet (Retrieved 11 September 2019)

Economics

Simon, David Robinson. *Meatonomics: how the rigged economy of meat and dairy make you consume too much — and how to eat better, live longer and spend smarter.* Conari Press, 2013

Environment

Nhat Hanh, Thich. *The World We Have: A Buddhist Approach to Peace and Ecology.* Parallax Press, 2004.

Supreme Master Ching Hai. *From Crisis to Peace: The Organic Vegan Way is The Answer.* Download e-book version free from http://crisis2peace.org/

https://www.health.govt.nz/system/files/documents/publications/sustainability-and-the-health-sector-30jul2019_1.pdf (Retrieved 16 October 2019)

Ethics

Thiroux, Jacques P and Krasemann, Keith W, *Ethics: Theory and Practice. 11th Ed.* Pearson Education, 2012

History

Joseph, Frank. *Atlantis and the Other Lost Worlds.* Arcturus, 2008

Huxley, Aldous, *Brave New World*, Penguin Books, 1932

Orwell, George. *Nineteen Eighty Four*, Penguin Books, 1949

Plato, *Timaeus/Critias*

Leadership

Pearson, Sharon. *Disruptive Leadership. Global Success Institute*, 2015

K-Burr, Betska. The Brain Walk. Free mindset tool available from www. TheBrainWalk.com

Ban Ki Moon. Remarks at the opening of the exhibit of the Chinese artist, Wu Weishan https://www.un.org/sg/en/content/sg/speeches/2012-09-04/remarks-opening-exhibit-chinese-artist-wu-weishan. (Retrieved 26 June 2019)

Mann, Clare. *Communicate: How To Say What Needs To Be Said When It Needs To Be Said In The Way It Needs To Be Said.* Communicate 31, 2012

Media

Australian Vegans Journal Download free PDF editions at www.AustralianVegans.com.au

Noteworthy News on Supreme Master Television Daily streaming free at www.SupremeMasterTV.com/NWN

Live Kindly www.livekindly.com

Jane Unchained https://janeunchained.com

Peace

https://reliefweb.int/report/world/global-peace-index-2019 (Retrieved 28 June 2019)

https://reliefweb.int/sites/reliefweb.int/files/resources/GPI-2019-web003.pdf (Retrieved 28 June 2019)

Politics

Baylis, John and Smith, Steve. *The Globalisation of World Politics*. 3rd Edition. Oxford University Press, 2005.

Williamson, Marianne. *The Politics of Love*. HarperCollins, 2019

Science and Technology

Bartlett, Jamie. *The People vs Tech*. Ebury Press, 2018

Spengler, Oswald. *The Decline of the West*. Alfred A. Knopf, 1932

Spiritual

Blavatsky, Helena P. *The Secret Doctrine* I and II.
Download free from www.theosociety.org

Bro, Harmon Hartzell. *Edgar Cayce. A Seer Out of Season*. The Aquarian Press, 1994..

Cannon, Dolores. *The Convoluted Universe*. Book Two. Ozark Mountain Publishing, 2005.

Rodwell, Mary. *The New Human: Awakening Our Cosmic Heritage*. New Mind Publishers, 2016

Supreme Master Ching Hai. *The Key Of Immediate Enlightenment*. Free download from http://www.smchbooks.com/new-eng/ebook/index.htm

Tzu, Lao. *Tao Te Ching*. *www.taoism.net* Free download available from website.

Veganism

Mann, Clare. *Vystopia: The Anguish of Being Vegan in a Non-Vegan World*. Communicate 31, 2018

Tuttle, Will. *The World Peace Diet: Eating for Spiritual Health and Social Harmony*. Lantern Books, 2005

Chapter References

This is a small sample of the references used in the writing of this book.

Chapter One

https://www.thelondoneconomic.com/opinion/economic-growth-is-an-unnecessary-evil-jacinda-ardern-is-right-to-deprioritise-it/ (Retrieved 4 March 2020)

https://www.globalcitizen.org/en/content/first-female-president-slovakia-caputova (Retrieved 4 March 2020)

https://www.weforum.org/agenda/2019/05/africa-is-leading-the-world-in-plastic-bag-bans (Retrieved 29 October 2019)

https://www.reuters.com/article/us-germany-energy-coal/germany-to-phase-out-coal-by-2038-in-move-away-from-fossil-fuels-idUSKCN1PK04L (Retrieved 4 March 2020)

https://www.niulife.com.au/erasing-poverty (Retrieved 4 March 2020)

https://www.independent.co.uk/news/world/asia/philippines-tree-planting-students-graduation-law-environment-a8932576.html (Retrieved 4 March 2020)

https://gulfnews.com/opinion/op-eds/towards-a-new-islamic-golden-age-1.1654232
(Retrieved 7 August 2019)

https://pal.ps/en/ (Retrieved 29 October 2019)

https://www.forbes.com/sites/trevornace/2019/02/28/nasa-says-earth-is-greener-today-than-20-years-ago-thanks-to-china-india (Retrieved, 29 October 2019)

Chapter Two

Future of Food

https://www.livekindly.co/new-zealand-just-urged-the-entire-country-to-eat-plant-based/
(Retrieved 28 October 2019)

https://www.health.govt.nz/publication/sustainability-and-health-sector
(Retrieved 28 October 2019)

https://www.veganaustralia.org.au/moving_to_a_vegan_agricultural_system_for_australia
(Retrieved 8 October 2019)

https://www.theguardian.com/environment/shortcuts/2019/sep/23/should-meat-be-banned-save-planet-new-laws-environment (Retrieved 4 March 2020)

https://www.livekindly.com/iceland-worlds-most-vegan-friendly-country
(Retrieved 7 August 2019)

https://www.independent.co.uk/news/uk/home-news/universal-basic-income-scotland-week-cash-payment-life-nicola-sturgeon-first-minister-snp-a7934131.html (Retrieved 7 August 2019)

https://www.weforum.org/agenda/2019/03/climate-change-is-a-security-threat-let-us-act-now (Retrieved 16 July 2019)

https://amp.smh.com.au/politics/federal/it-was-only-ever-going-to-end-one-way-how-richo-sealed-nsw-alp-s-fate-20190901-p52mrr.html (Sean Kelly quote)
(Retrieved 21 September 2019)

https://www.ted.com/talks/nicola_sturgeon_why_governments_should_prioritize_well_being/details (Retrieved September 21 2019)

https://www.vice.com/en_us/article/bj9yjq/the-radical-plan-to-save-the-planet-

by-working-less
(Retrieved 4 March 2020)

https://www.theguardian.com/australia-news/2020/jan/14/a-billion-animals-the-australian-species-most-at-risk-from-the-bushfire-crisis (Retrieved 19 January 2020)

https://www.livekindly.co/bezos-branson-gates-vegan-meat-investment-motif (Retrieved 28th April 2020)

Environment

Arsenault, C. 'Only 60 Years of Farming Left If Soil Degradation Continues.' *Scientific American Journal*, December 5, 2014.

Woinarski, J., Murphy, B., Nimmmo, D., Braby, M.F., Legge, S., Garnett, S. 'Scientists Re-Counted Australia's Extinct Species. And The Result Is Devastating". *Live Science Journal*, December 2, 2019.

Bakker, E.S., and Svenning, J-C.'Trophic rewilding: consequences for ecosystems under global change', *The Royal Society Journal*, 22nd October 2018.

Clark, M.A., Springmann, M., Hill, J., Tillman, D. 2019. 'Multiple health and environmental impacts of foods.' *Proceedings of the National Academy of Sciences*, Oct 2019

Herring, R. and Wirick, R. *The Need to Grow*, 2019.

Monbiot, George. *Feral: Rewilding the Land, the Sea, and Human Life*. University of Chicago Press, 2017

Science and Technology

https://www.theguardian.com/science/2019/aug/03/first-human-monkey-chimera-raises-concern-among-scientists (Retrieved 4 March 2020)

https://7news.com.au/sunrise/on-the-show/microchipped-couple-open-doors-and-turn-on-lights-with-a-flick-of-their-wrists-c-396865.amp? (Retrieved 4 March 2020)

https://bigthink.com/videos/ray-kurzweil-on-the-future-of-nanotechnology (Retrieved 4 March 2020)

Chapter Three

https://www.globalcitizen.org/en/content/canadian-nominee-childrens-peace-prize (Retrieved 19th January 2020)

https://thisisafrica.me/politics-and-society/african-vegans-return-tradition/ (Retrieved 19th January 2020)

https://www.saveur.com/africas-vegetable-roots/ (Retrieved 19th January 2020)

https://www.lexico.com/en/definition/rhetoric

https://wearyourvoicemag.com/news-politics/youth-climate-activists-of-color (Retrieved 19th January 2020)

Your Notes

Other titles by
Kathy Divine

∞

Kathy Divine's books are available from all major online book stores in both print and digital formats. Available from Amazon here:

https://amzn.to/2vDTs3T

To download your free copies of Kathy's magazine, Australian Vegans Journal, please visit
www.AustralianVegans.com.au

About the Author
Kathy Divine

∞

Kathy Divine is the author of six books, the founder of *Australian Vegans Journal* and the Plant-Powered Women Leadership Conference Series, and coaches aspiring authors. Kathy grew up in a political family and lived and breathed politics as a child. She has adhered to a daily meditation practice for 23 years. Kathy has contemplated deeply on the subjects of politics and spirituality throughout her life and over time developed the framework for *Golden Age Politics*.

Kathy offers two coaching services:

1. coaching aspiring authors through the entire publishing process; and
2. coaching leaders (and aspiring leaders) in mindset and personal branding

Kathy offers one-on-one coaching sessions and coaching through her online programs

Please visit www.kathydivine.com/mentor for details

Kathy Divine

AUTHOR ✦ MENTOR